First published in Great Britain in 2016 by A Way With Media Ltd, Shrewsbury, SY3 7LN

Copyright © Anand George 2016

A CIP catalogue record for this book is available from the British Library.

ISBN 978-1910-469-064

Photography, editor, publisher: Andy Richardson

Editorial production, design: David Briggs

Printed and bound by 1010 Printing International Ltd, China.

www.awaywithmedia.com

Purple Poppadom,
185a Cowbridge Road East, Cardiff, CF11 9AJ
TEL: 029 2022 0026
🐦 @ChefAnandGeorge
www.purplepoppadom.com

This book is dedicated to my beloved
father Vengacheril Joseph George

Forewords

I remember some years ago there being a buzz on the food scene in Cardiff with talk of a newly opened Indian restaurant, Mint and Mustard. This restaurant was the platform that introduced us to Anand George, a hot new talent from Kerala, who was quickly carving out a reputation for himself in producing cutting-edge Indian cuisine, the like of which Cardiff had never experienced before.

Naturally I made it my business to go and investigate. I knew instantly when I saw the menu content that we were in for a treat. Just the way it read was a far cry from the style of Indian cuisine I had grown up with and I was eager to explore this new offering and find out more about the man behind this new wave of exciting dishes.

Ordering was difficult, what to choose? I waited eagerly for the first course of street food style snacks to arrive – it did not disappoint, everything was so delicious, fragrant and beautifully balanced and impeccably presented. From that moment on I knew I would become good friends with this chef.

Since those early days, Anand has blossomed into a restaurateur in his own right opening The Purple Poppadom, winning rave reviews and establishing a loyal following of fans. I remember urging Jay Rayner to visit the restaurant (which we did after recording one of his radio shows in Cardiff), he loved it and penned a very worthy review, which was so deserved and I was thrilled for Anand.

This man is high energy, he's focused and determined. As well as running PP, you can also find him fronting numerous pop-up restaurants, running street food stalls, demonstrating at events, lending his talents to charity events and running cookery classes, the list goes on – and now a book.

The book is beautiful and a real testament to just how far he has come and the adventures that lay ahead for him in the culinary world. His generosity is present on every page as he shares with us his personal stories, memories and influences. His expertise in relating his comprehensive repertoire of recipes is done with great ease, which conveys the measure of talent in this man.

I am honoured to know him, on occasion, to work with him and am looking forward to the next chapter he unfolds.

Angela Gray, from Angela Gray's Cookery School

As a proud Welshman, I feel truly blessed to live in a country where the produce is second to none. We are a nation of great producers and great chefs; we respect nature's bountiful harvest each time we enter our kitchens. We respect our proud heritage and embrace the future as we seek to create new gastronomic experiences for our diners.

I have come to know and respect Chef Anand as both a talented chef and good friend. We have cooked together on several occasions and I have been captivated by his exceptional understanding of flavours.

His Keralan dishes have dazzled customers, his authentic flavours have stayed long in the memory and his technical ability is outstanding.

As Wales develops as a culinary nation, it needs men like Anand George to carry things forward. He is at the cutting-edge with vibrant dishes that add playfulness and deliciousness to our table.

Anand and I have cooked together on numerous occasions, creating East meets West gourmet evenings that have delighted diners. They have always been enormous fun and I have the greatest respect for his ability.

As a chef, collaborating with other cooks is not always easy. There might be a difference of ideas or opinion, a clash of styles or a disagreement over how to use a particular ingredient.

Yet when two chefs find themselves on the same page, the magic happens. And I love working with Anand because he always brings something different to the table. He introduces elements of cuisine that my guests might be unaccustomed to, including a whole host of new spices and ingredients.

Those techniques and ingredients are featured in Anand's debut book. It is a remarkable title that chronicles his 5,000 mile journey and reveals the inspiration for his work. We are proud that Anand has become an adopted son of Wales. And I have no doubt that his journey will continue.

James Sommerin, Restaurant James Sommerin

CONTENTS

My Story
Pages 13 - 37

Memories of my Father
Pages 38 - 41

History of Kochi
Pages 42 - 45

Recipes

Amuse Bouche – Starters
Pages 48 - 95

Four Ladies and One Chef
Pages 96 - 111

Fish
Pages 112 - 129

Meat

Pages 130 - 169

Vegetables

Pages 170 - 187

Street Food

Pages 188 - 201

Desserts

Pages 202 - 213

Base Recipes

Pages 214 - 225

Glossary and Ingredients

Pages 226 - 235

Index

Pages 236 - 237

MYSTORY

I love food. I am at my happiest when I'm creating new dishes. Nothing inspires me as much as that creative process. It thrills me every day.

We are the product of our environment and the more I consider my culinary story, the more I realise everything I do is inspired by the country of my birth, the role of my parents, my family and friends. They formed and informed me from my earliest years to the present day.

I was a bright boy when it came to school, though I wasn't always the hardest worker. In fact, there were times when I was quite lazy. But my parents encouraged me. They taught me that you had to have a good education to get on in life. In Kerala, it was survival of the fittest. You had to pass your exams otherwise you would amount to nothing. So my mother used to make me sit in the kitchen to make sure I did my homework.

Sometimes, my mind would drift. I'd sit there with a pen and a book but instead of paying attention to my books I would be watching what she was cooking. I wasn't allowed to get involved. The kitchen was my mother's domain and it was always full of incredible smells and aromas. They were beautiful.

My mother understood my love of food. She could see that I was excited by it. And so she would feed me generously. When everyone else ate one, I would have two. She reasoned the best thing to do to keep me happy and encourage me to study was to feed me.

As a boy, the thought of becoming a chef didn't enter my mind. I grew up in a culture where there was a clear delineation between responsibilities for men and women. Put simply, men rarely entered kitchens. My father, for instance, never wanted me to become a chef. When I finished my graduation in commerce, he told me to join a bank where I could get a decent job. Cooking was a profession that was not highly regarded. But now things have changed. When I return to Kerala now, I am welcomed as a celebrity chef. Things have changed.

But not all change is good. We lose some things along the way. As the world moves more quickly and life becomes ever-faster, we lose some of the fine things in life. Our culture becomes eroded.

We might be living in smart cities and have access to life's luxuries, but we pay a high price.

My mother's kitchen back home in Kerala was my school room and restaurant trips with my father were like visiting lecture theatres. In both cases, my parents were my teachers guiding me through my earliest experiences of food.

I often think how blessed I was to be born in Kerala. It was incredibly diverse and its remarkable environment lent itself to an abundant store cupboard of ingredients. Kerala offered coastline and inland waterways, bountiful paddy fields and rich pastures. Its climate was conducive to a treasure trove of herbs and spices. That gastronomic heritage inspires me each day. It leaves me constantly searching for new combinations and adventures for my customers' tastebuds.

In this book my mission is to share with you my experiences, my 5,000-mile journey. It took me from Kerala, where I was born and learned about food, to the UK, where I developed my own take on cuisine.

As a chef I like to reference the cuisine of Kerala and the different parts of India in which I worked. But my stints in international kitchens exposed me to different cooking techniques from France, Britain and other parts of the world. They all have a part to play in my modern Indian cuisine.

By birth I am a Syrian Christian, which meant that many meals at home included pork and beef, meat that my friends from other religions were not permitted to eat.

Food was heavily featured in our festivals. Onam, our festival of harvest, was rooted in Hinduism, but was celebrated by all Malayalees, a term used to describe people of Kerala from all cultures and religions.

Inevitably, a lot of dishes were based on rice. Kerala had a tremendous amount of rice cultivation so rice was a staple. Since it was surrounded by water, fish were particularly abundant, like karimeen or pearl spot, mackerel and sardine. But the most interesting part in cooking fish was using an exotic ingredient called kodumpuli, or fish tamarind. It's a yellow, tree-grown fruit that is sun-dried and salt smoked. It gives a tangy sourness to fish curries and cuts through any fishy taste.

Keralan food sometimes felt like medicine with anti-oxidant-rich dishes helping to cleanse the body. Karkidaka Marunnu Kanji, medicinal porridge, was taken in the Malayalam month of Karkidakam (the Ramayana months of July-August). It was rainy season in Kerala and no agricultural work

could be performed. A herbal concoction was used to purify the body and soul. It had a wonderful rejuvenating effect. I distinctly remember Injipuli, ginger chutney, too. While it tasted beautiful, it also had restorative effects because it was packed with vitamins and minerals.

Many dishes that I ate as a child featured ingredients that had no apparent role. They didn't add a flavour or texture and I often wondered why they were there. But the answer wasn't so hard to find. The process of adding ash gourd, into olan (a dish prepared with ash gourd, coconut milk, ginger and coconut oil), for instance, was all about promoting health. The dish was served as a part of sadhya and the ash gourd had a cooling effect, worked as a laxative and also flushed toxins from the body. Keralan cuisine was built on being healthy as well as being flavoursome.

Now, sad to say, it's not the same. The important ingredients that kept people healthy are being lost. The older traditions are dying out.

When I was a boy, we ate fish curries, beef stews, pork vindaloo and so on. The food was a bit spicy because my father used to smoke and he needed extra spice to taste it.

Festivals and special occasions were dominated by food. At Christmas, we didn't think of the presents, we thought more about the food. Plum cake and homemade wine were followed by rice pancakes or bread with a huge beef stew. For lunch, we'd eat beef cutlet; a beef mince cooked with subtle spices mixed with mashed potatoes, bread crumbed and fried. There would also be beef coconut fry, pork vindaloo, meen policha curry then steamed rice and vegetables.

The traditional Kerala lunch, called sadhya, was a striking and dramatic presentation served on a giant banana leaf, with between 18 and 21 vegetarian dishes. It was accepted by all castes and religions.

Those religions were important and I remember Muslim family friends sharing 'Moplah' cuisine. A legacy of that cuisine is Malabar biryani, which is one of my favourite dishes. The dish can be made for between 1,000 and 5,000 guests at traditional Keralan weddings.

Inland waterways are a major feature of Kerala. Boats were the main mode of transport and the boatmen would cook on board as part of their everyday working life.

With the rise of tourism, those working boats have been converted into houseboats, like small floating hotels, where hosts try to replicate the old style of food for their guests. I have taken that inspiration to create a fish curry, though it uses monkfish and is more refined.

The city of Kochi, where I was born and grew up, is also known as Cochin. It is the upcoming metropolitan city of Kerala. It remains my spiritual home and there is a popular phrase 'Kochi is not a city; it's a feeling'. That is how it is for me. When I visit I feel at home, it energises me.

Kochi has been an important spice trading centre on the west coast of India since the 14th century and was sometimes referred to as the 'Queen of the Arabian Sea'. Centuries ago, traders would import new foods and cultures when they landed. Those were gradually amalgamated into the traditional dishes of indigenous people.

Beef stew, for example was introduced to the region by spice traders. But it was adapted by locals who added coconut milk and other ingredients like cinnamon, cardamom, cloves and peppercorns. That was how Keralan food developed. It was a hybridised fusion of styles.

There are other great examples of dishes that arose from Kerala's international heritage. Vindalu, for instance, was derived from the Portuguese carne de vinha d'alhos, which literally means meat, wine and garlic. Portuguese sailors who visited Kerala would preserve their raw produce in wooden barrels with alternate layers of pork and garlic and soaked in wine. That is how the dish originated. It was then transformed by local cooks who added palm vinegar, sugar, fresh ginger, mustard and spices.

In the UK vindaloo became known as a fiendishly hot curry house classic, far different from its origins. In our restaurants, however, we like to honour the original more-flavoursome style by using pork.

Keralan cooking at its best is an amalgam of wonderful influences from around the world.

It feels fitting that my journey brought me to England and Wales because the British Raj had a huge influence on our cooking.

The legacy of Anglo-Indian cuisine remains strong.

A good example of an Anglo-Indian signature dish is ball curry, which is made of mincemeat. It was very popular dish at weddings and became a staple as local people married into the families of colonial rulers. Roasted coconut paste was added to the minced meat balls to make them softer and giving them a nice nutty taste.

The use of eggs in our cooking was another legacy of the Raj, though we took that to new heights. My mother used to make an egg curry with boiled eggs with onion, tomato, coconut milk and spices. It is a dish that I have refined slightly by individually braising the eggs in the sauce. The eggs are served with string hoppers, also called idiyappam, which are rice noodles of Sri Lankan influence. The other addition was puttu, a dish of ground rice layered with coconut which is steamed in bamboo cylinders.

It took me a while to find my route into food. My father didn't want me to be a chef and during my teenage years my biggest preoccupation was

cricket, rather than cooking. I was a fast bowler and would have loved to play professionally. When I left school, at 15, I went to a college that had a good cricket team. I would cycle to school and then play as many cricket matches as I could.

When I graduated three years later, my parents were very happy. I had qualified in commerce and accountancy.

A lot of my friends tried to persuade me against cooking. They told me cooking was too tough, they said being a chef would kill me. I loved food, I loved eating food, it was such a big passion.

My move into the world of cuisine as a profession began in Aurangabad, where I attended culinary school and later graduated. I went on to work in many five star Indian hotels – in Delhi, Madras, Kerala, Rajasthan and Bombay. In those luxurious properties I developed culinary skills and learnt

how to cook on a large scale, often for many hundreds of guests at a time. From the North to the South, I developed an understanding of the many and varied cuisines of India.

One of the places in which I worked was the Taj Palace Hotel, in Delhi. It was a 440-room hotel and I was sent there for six months to complete my training. The exposure was great because it taught me other skills. It was a major banqueting hotel and it would do conference lunches for 5,000 guests and dinner for 10,000. I got exposed to North Indian cuisine and it was the best place to get the basics right. The days were long, from 7am till midnight. Around that time, I lost my father, and I decided to go back to Kochi. The chefs I worked with would start at 9am, but I would start at 7am and I pushed as hard as I could.

One of the jobs that I had to do was grate coconut. On a good day I would do 70-80 coconuts with a grinder. It was a terrible machine and I had to use it correctly otherwise it would cut off my hand. By going into work at 7am, I gave myself the time to get everything done before the others arrived. I started getting confidence from Chef Anil Kumar, who gave me the opportunity to cook. I served the staff food, moved onto buffets and learned how to cook for 100 people. Again, it built my confidence. All the while, I wanted to learn how to use my hands so that I could cook better. I wasn't interested in just doing the donkey work, I wanted to cook. My passion, of course, was for the food of Kerala. It's what I'd grown up with and what I loved most.

It is interesting that it took a relocation to the UK on my 5,000 mile culinary journey to realise my new take on traditional Indian cuisine.

My springboard was the London restaurant scene, which included working in a Michelin star restaurant, Zaika. That proved to me that a more experimental approach to Indian cuisine would work well.

I started at Zaika in February 2005 and it took my breath away. The team there had a different way of doing things. Before arriving, I'd been running the pass with a brigade of 12 staff. I'd been in a management position but at Zaika I was back to square one working as a commis. Everything was different. There were six of us in the kitchen and it was work, work, work. They even put me on pastry, a section I'd never have chosen in my life.

I did a couple of months there and worked with new techniques. I developed one of my signature desserts, a chocolate samosa, after

experimenting with their Paco Jet. Zaika gave me a completely different outlook. Zaika had been created by Chef Vineet Bhatia who changed the perception of Indian fine dining in UK. He is a man of great innovation. His example was the one I followed. The fact that he had built something up to be so successful encouraged me to be innovative and to follow my vision.

My urge to redefine, is by no means a slur on the cuisine of my country. For me classic dishes remain essential and should always be celebrated.

However, there is room to modify and develop. Just as the cuisine of Kerala was transformed over centuries by culture, trade and religion, so we should continue our evolutionary journey.

Having learned new skills in the UK I opened my first restaurant, Mint and Mustard, Cardiff.

Initially, we started with a simple menu and slowly I built a team and started to refine Anglo-Indian food. With my experience from Kerala, Rajasthan, Chennai, Delhi, Bombay and London, I started something that was completely new. Some of our customers came in expecting Mint and Mustard to be just another back street curry house. But they soon started to learn that we were all about refinement. We would have guests come in ask for a biryani and a curry sauce. I would say: 'No, I don't do that', and some would walk out. But I stuck to my guns.

Mint and Mustard was a hit. By 2009 it was named as one of the Best 100 Restaurants in the UK.

It won entry into the Good Food Guide and the Michelin guide and I was invited to demonstrate at the Abergavenny Food Festival, which is one of the biggest in the UK.

I also cooked Britain's most expensive curry. There was a charity auction in 2010 and two bidders fought over me. One bid to £14,000 but the other went to £15,000. The guy who was running the auction asked if I'd cook at both and I agreed. It was the highest price they'd ever got and the record still stands.

In 2011, I opened Purple Poppadom. The crowds came flocking. Purple Poppadom soon earned a reputation across the region. It earned a place in Hardens, Michelin and the Good Food Guide. The thing that set us apart was our flavours and our sense of refinement. Some of the lessons I'd learned at Zaika, about textures, presentation and flavour, were brought

to the fore.

We also looked to improve the quality of our menu. We introduced head-to-tail cooking, using pig heads and offal. The food reflected my 5,000-mile journey. I have been influenced by food from around the world, by the Keralan food that was itself influenced by travellers from Portugal and other parts of the world. I love subtle food and that's what we serve at our outlets.

A lot of Indian food is over-spiced, it is killed by too much heat so that you can't taste the chicken or beef or lamb. But I try not to overkill it. I like the spices to be subtle. I also like to use different cuts of meat, rather than just fillet, because they impart different flavours and textures.

Since arriving in the UK, I have twice entered the Tiffin Cup and I have twice won it.

My strength is cooking and I stick to that. I love food, it brings me great joy – and I hope that in cooking it for others I can bring them great joy too. For me food is ultimately a sharing experience and my aim is to create dishes that both excite and intrigue.

I hope the recipes in this book will introduce you to my world of modern Indian cuisine.

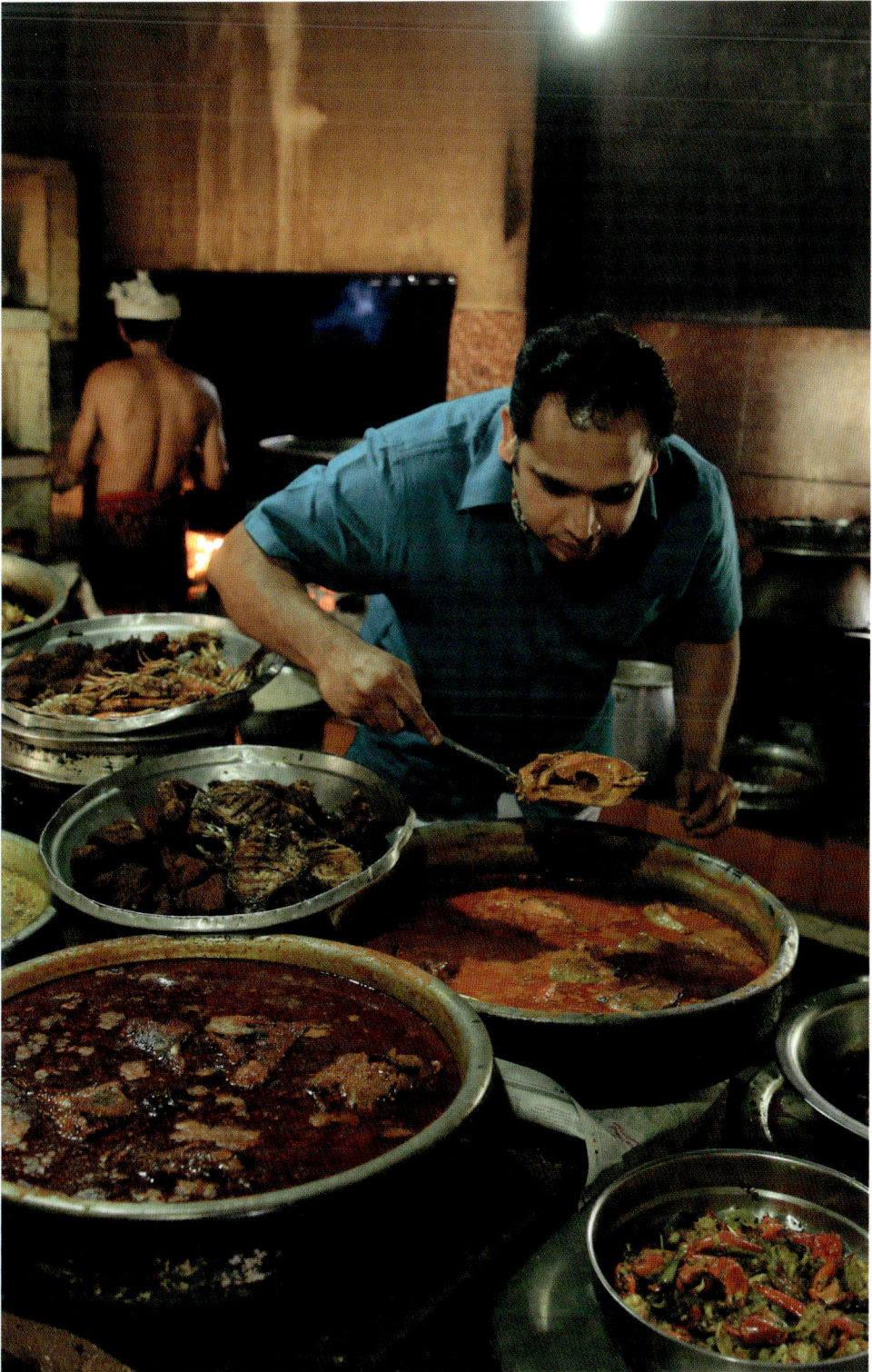

Anand George **37**

Memories of my Father

The journey from Kochi to Kuttanad, in Alleppey, stirs memories of my father. It was his native place and it would take us a quarter of a day to travel in a taxi from Kochi to Ramangiri before transferring to a vallam (a paddled long boat) and continuing our journey. We would eventually arrive at my grandmother's house, where the terrain was rural and remote.

Lives were lived at the water's edge and while our boat sailed by, little children dived and splashed in the water. Mothers washed clothes and gutted fish for their afternoon meal.

After an hour-and-a-half of travelling, we would reached the Vengacherry Tharavadu (our family house). The vista was stunning with a paddy field and water stream in front of the house.

When lunch was served it featured large dishes of soft red rice, beef stir

fried with coconut, roast duck, fiery red fish curry and vegetables like avial, thoran and buttermilk along with pickles. During evening, cups of sweet tea and tins of palaharams (goodies) were served, including sugary, frosted cheeda, savoury kuzhalappam, grainy cones of churuttu, achappam or rose cookies and avalosunda.

Such memories remind me that the smells and tastes of Kerala have been with me since I was just a boy. Food was a big part of my growing up and my earliest memories were dominated by it. The same was true of my father and, I imagine, of his father too.

My father had five children, I was the youngest and my elders were Asha, Amita, Ashita and Anupama. Father would tell me about his school years and his memories often focused on lunchtimes. His own father was the headmaster of a school and my father used to travel there on a snake boat. Snake boats are very small and my father's would be followed by an additional snake boat that would carry rice, fish, pulses and other ingredients. My father also loved food and recalled on many times the food he ate.

The masters at my father's school were always very particular about their daily menu. Food was to be appreciated and enjoyed, rather than used for sustenance. My father ate freshly-cooked lunches each day. That was the culture that he came from and I guess that's where my culinary story begins. My father passed his love of food down to me. His gastronomic experiences were based on quality, rather than quantity.

I was born in 1977 and grew up in Kerala, just like my father. He'd grown up in Alleppey, the granary of Kerala, where there was abundant rice cultivation. My father later moved to Kochi and he was a mature man, aged 48, by the time I came along.

He moved to Kochi to advance his entrepreneurial skills.

When my father and I spent time together, food would always feature. He expressed his affection for me through food. He would take me to restaurants, it was his way of communicating his love. I went from as early as I can remember. My peers would play sport with their fathers, or go out for the day. But I don't remember ever going with my father to a circus or a movie; instead, it was always to a restaurant.

Often, my father would tell me stories about old toddy shops, the places where people would drink, or about places he'd eaten or drunk. He didn't take me to a toddy shop, of course, but he would take me to small cafes or buy food and bring it home.

My father would bring home unusual things like oxtail during monsoon times, and my mother would make soup. I still remember the earthen soup pot which bubbled away over a wood fire. Mother's food was tasty, nourishing and had the same restorative effect as medicine.

My father had great dress sense. He had an honest and daring personality. As a boy, he would provide me with work so that I could earn money and become a man. He would send me to the post office to send money orders or to the bank so that I could draw a cheque or make a draft. Doing those tasks gave me independence and freedom. I would also do a lot of home sales, going door to door with various products, which built my confidence. The experience made me increasingly enterprising.

Once I'd left home and ventured into the culinary world, my father kept in touch by writing letters to me. He passed away before I finished my catering college, but his grace is around me and guides me through my journey. I love him dearly.

History of Kochi

Long before the time of Christ, spice merchants and travellers from around the world visited Kerala. The important seaport of Muziris, or Cranganore, was populated with Greeks, Syrians, Jews, and Chinese traders who lived in harmony with people of the region. It was on one of those trading vessels, plying between Alexandria and the Malabar Coast, that Saint Thomas, the apostle landed at Muziris, the premier seaport of South India about the year 52 A.D. and founded seven churches on the Malabar coast.

Among these early conversions were several Namboodiri families, from whom many of the present–day Syrian Christians trace their roots, including my own family.

Rise of Cochin or the present Kochi

If the history of the Ernakulum District from the 9th to the 12th centuries is interlinked with that of the Kulasekharas of Mahodayapuram, its history since the 12th century is the history of the rise and growth of Perumpadappu Swarupam (Cochin State).

Cochin port is believed to have developed only as late as 1341. As the result of a heavy flood in the Periyar, the ancient harbour of Muziris became silted and useless for the purposes of trade.

This seems to be a convincing explanation for the absence of any reference to Cochin in earlier foreign notices of Malabar. Cochin soon rose in prominence and the commercial supremacy enjoyed by Cranganore passed to Cochin. The rulers of Perumpadappu Swarupam shifted their headquarters from Mahodayapuram and established it in Cochin early in the 15th Century. In the 13th and 14th century, Zamorins considerably increased their power and became masters of a vast dominion in Northern and Central Kerala.

For about a century-and-a-half after the formation of the harbour, Cochin was a premium port on the west coast and carried on a brisk trade with China, Arabia, Persia and the coastal towns of western India.

Beginning of the Conflict between Cochin and Calicut

In the 13th and 14th century Arabs merchants settled in large numbers. They helped the Zamorin with men and money to expand his dominion at the expense of the petty chiefs. By the beginning of 15th Century the Zamorin had grown in power and prestige and acquired superiority over the ruler of Cochin.

Cochin on eve of the Portuguese arrival

Toward the close of the 15th century The Elaya Thavazhi of Perumpadappu Swarupam was holding the reins of power. The Mootha Thavazhi, which resented that, sought help from the Zamorin against the reigning Raja. Zamorin marched to the south end with a large army and defeated the

Raja and occupied his palace at Trichur. He installed his partisan on the Cochin throne. The new ruler accepted the Zamorin suzerainty and undertook to pay him an annual tribute.

Accompanied by a Portuguese gentleman Michael Jogue interviewed the Cochin Raja. The Raja received the emissary with great friendliness and expressed himself in favour of the Portuguese, being allowed to purchase from Cochin whatever they want.

The Cochin Raja granted permission to the Portuguese to build a factory at Cochin while the Portuguese promised to free the Raja of the Zamorin yoke and even to add Calicut to his dominion at some future date. Portuguese sailors loaded the ship with rich merchandise. Prior to his departure the Cochin Raja entrusted to Cabral a letter of friendship written in golden leaf to the king of Portugal.

Cabral's activities at Cochin constitute the first chapter in the history of European contact with the place. Joao Da Nova the next Portuguese captain who arrived at Cochin (in 1501) had to meet the hostility of the Zamorin during his expedition and the King of Portugal who became indignant on receipt of this information sent a fleet of ships under Vasco Da Gama to retaliate against the Zamorin and establish Portuguese supremacy in the Arabian sea. After bombarding Calicut and annihilating the Arab Merchant fleets on the way, Vasco Da Gama arrived at Cochin on 7th November 1502.

The Portuguese where allowed by the Raja to load their ships with merchandise. Da Gama, however, behaved in an imperious manner in his dealings with the Raja and dictated to him the terms for an alliance.

Pepper, cardamom and other spices were to be sold to the Portuguese at a price to be fixed by the Admiral. The Portuguese were also to be given the exclusive right of building factories and keeping garrisons at places of their choice in Cochin. The Raja accepted the terms without protest and Da Gama gave him valuable presents including a gold crown.

The Portuguese triumphs at Cochin alarmed the Zamorin of Calicut.

With victories in Cochin and Cranganore the Portuguese had won the first round of their fight in Kerala. It became clear that there was no possibility of driving them away from the Indian Coast. They gained the right to trade; and by the relations entered in to with Cochin, Quilon and Cannanore, they had secured considerable commercial interests. Neither on sea, nor on land were they masters; but the Moors, the Zamorin and other Indian powers recognised after four years of fighting that a new and incalculable factor had been added to the already complicated politics of India.

Effects of Portuguese rule

The Portuguese left traces of their influence in the economic, social and cultural fields. They also secured a world market for Indian goods, especially spices. They introduced into India a number of new products and the most important was the cashew tree (still known in Kerala as Parangi Mavu). Tobacco was another product which they introduced and cultivated on a large scale. They also bought in tropical fruits from South America – the custard apple, guava, pineapple and papaya. They introduced the scientific cultivation of pepper, ginger and coconuts, and even brought in the seed nuts of a better and bigger type of coconut from Africa. Cochin grew into a large and flourishing commercial town and became, after Goa, the finest and the largest city in the Malabar coast.

The Portuguese built the Mattancherri Palace about 1555 and presented it to the ruler, Vira Kerala Varma, who withdrew the ban imposed early on in the Portuguese period on conversions to Christianity in the Cochin Kingdom. In 1565 the Jews left Cranganore en masse as a result of Portuguese prosecution and settled down at Cochin and Ernakulam. To the south of the Raja's Palace in Mattancherri, they built in 1567 what came to be called in later years the "Jew Town".

Dutch Cochin

The Dutch conquest of Cochin occured in January 1663. The Dutch East India Company began to dispatch ships to India from 1595 onwards and through many encounters with the Portuguese and their allies the Dutch succeeded in establishing their power in several places in India and Ceylon. Having established themselves as the masters of Cochin the Dutch made it their headquarters in Kerala. The Dutch improved the agricultural economy of Kerala by introducing better methods of coconut cultivation, also taking it to a larger scale in order to meet the increasing demand for coir and coconut oil. To the Dutch goes the abiding honour of having compiled the Hortus Malabaricus, the famous work on Indian Botany which deals in detail with the medicinal properties of Indian plants. Several years of labour were spent completing this monumental work and it was finally published in Amsterdam between 1686 and 1703 in twelve volumes with 794 nicely executed copper plate engravings. In compiling the Hortus Malabricus the Dutch received help from several scholars, both native and European. The most prominent of the native scholars associated with this work were three Brahmins named Ranga Bhat, Vinayak Pandit and Appu Bhat and an Ezhava by the name of Itti Achuthan. Apart from the Dutch Governor Van Rheede, who took personal interest in its compilation, the most prominent of the European scholars associated with this project was the Carmelite Mathaeus, a highly educated monk.

To Present Day

In accordance with the Anglo-Dutch Treaty of 1814, the islands of Kochi, including Fort Kochi and its territory, were ceded to the UK in exchange for the island of Banca.

Even prior to the signing of this treaty, there is evidence of English residents in Cochin. By the early 20th century, trade at Cochin port had increased substantially and the need to develop the port was greatly felt. Over a span of 21 years, Cochin was transformed into the safest harbour in the peninsula, where ships berthed alongside the newly reclaimed inner harbour, which was equipped with a long array of steam cranes.

In 1866, Fort Cochin was made a municipality. Cochin was the first princely state to willingly join the Indian Union when India gained independence in 1947. Cochin merged with Travancore to create Travancore-Cochin, which was in turn merged with the Malabar district of Madras State on 1 November 1956 to form the new Indian state of Kerala.

Recipes

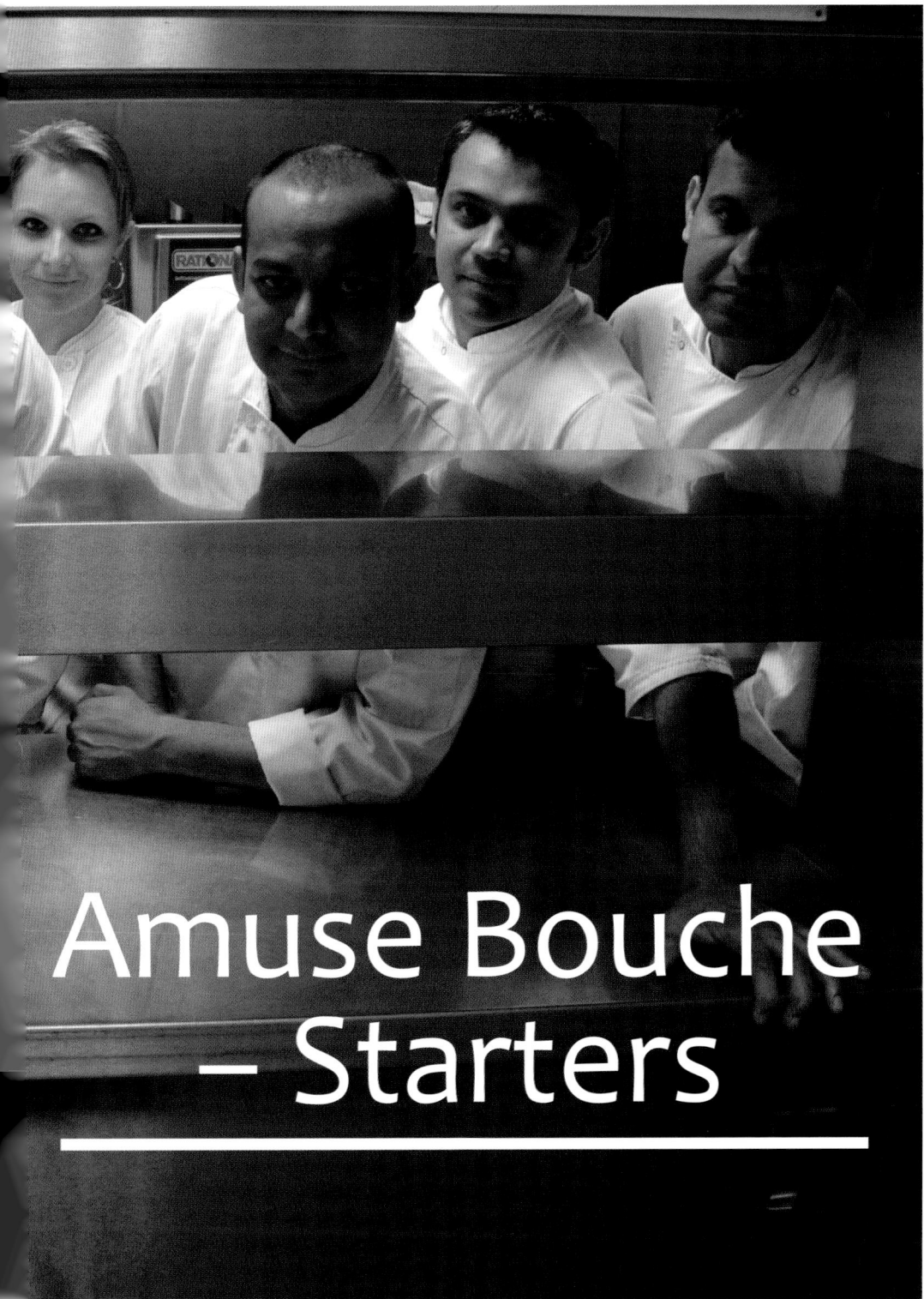

Amuse Bouche – Starters

COCONUTSO UPAND CABBAGECAKE

Cabbage Cake

What you'll need

Portion 24 piece x 30gms
White Cabbage – 475gms (one small cabbage)
Oil – 25ml
Red onions – 50gms
Ginger – 4gms
Green chilli – 2gms
Cumin seeds – 2gms
Salt – 8gms
Turmeric powder – 2gms

Cumin powder – 6gms
Lemon juice – 15ml
Chat masala – 4gms
Sugar – 3gms
Fresh coriander leaves – 6gms
Grated potatoes– 350gms (base recipe)
Eggs
Breadcrumbs
Oil to fry

How it's done

1. Remove any damaged outer leaves of the cabbage. Rinse and dry. Cut the cabbage into quarters over a stable cutting board.
2. Remove the white core and chop the cabbage finely.
3. Subsequently chop the red onions, ginger, green chilli and coriander leaves.
4. Heat oil in a pan, add cumin seeds. As it starts popping add the ginger, green chilli and red onions; sauté it for 2-3 mins on a low heat. Add salt, turmeric powder, cumin powder; saute for a minute.
5. Add the chopped cabbage and stir fry it for 3-4 mins. Finish with lemon juice, chat masala, sugar and fresh coriander.
6. Allow the mixture to cool and mix it with the grated potato. Divide it into 24 balls of 30gms each and shape into small cakes.
7. Beat the eggs, dip the cabbage cake in the beaten egg, breadcrumbs and fry in oil.

Coconut Soup

What you'll need

Portion 12 x 60ml
Coconut oil – 25ml
Mustard seeds –1gm
Urad dal split – 1gm
Green chilli –4gms
Whole ginger – 20gms
Whole garlic – 20gms
Curry leaves –2gms
Salt – 6gms
Asafoetida powder – 1gm
Coconut milk powder – 125gms
Sugar – 2gms
Crushed black pepper – 2gms
Cardamom powder – 1gm
Tomato chutney (base recipe)

How it's done

1. Mix coconut milk powder with 750ml of luke warm water and blend it.
2. Wash and slice ginger with the skin still on. Slice the garlic with the peel on and slit the green chilli.
3. Heat oil in a pan, add urad dal and allow it to pop then add the mustard seeds and let it crackle.
4. Add ginger, garlic, green chilli and curry leaves. As soon it turns light brown, lower the heat. Add asafoetida powder and salt, pour the coconut milk in the pan and bring to it boil. Keep stirring to avoid it sticking to the bottom.
5. Let it simmer for 7-8 mins and finish it with sugar, crushed black pepper and cardamom powder.
6. Allow the soup to enhance the flavour, leave it for an half an hour then pass it through a fine sieve.
7. Serve hot.

BEETROOTCAKEAND DALSHORBA

Beetroot Cake

What you'll need

Portion – 24 piece x 30gms
Oil to fry
Beetroot – 300gms
Carrot – 220gms
Ginger – 10gms
Green chilli – 4gms
Curry leaves –2gms
Onions – 170gms
Salt – 8gms

Turmeric powder – 2gms
Coriander powder – 5gms
Kashmiri chilli powder – 2gms
Oil – 25ml
Garam masala – 2gms
Crushed black peppercorns – 2gms
Grated potatoes – 330gms (base recipe)
Eggs
Breadcrumbs

How it's done

1. Peel beetroot and carrot and finely chop.
2. Chop onions, ginger, green chilli and curry leaves.
3. Heat oil in a pan, add ginger, green chilli, curry leaves and onions. Sauté for 2-3 mins.
4. Reduce the flame and add turmeric powder, coriander powder, Kashmiri chilli powder and salt. Place the chopped beetroot and carrot, and saute for 3-4 mins. Don't overcook. The beetroot and carrot should both still have crunch.
5. Finally sprinkle the crushed black peppercorns and garam masala. Take off the heat and allow the mixture to cool.
6. Combined the cooled mixture with the grated potatoes and divide into 24 balls of 30gms each, shaping like a cake.
7. Beat the eggs, dip the beetroot cake in the beaten egg, breadcrumbs and fry in oil.

Dal Shorba

What you'll need

Portion 20 x 60ml
Masoor dal – 150gms (red lentil)
Water – 1.5 litre
Salt – 12gms
Coriander powder – 2gms
Cumin powder – 2gms
Turmeric powder – 2gms
Coriander leaf stems – 40gms
Tomatoes – 90gms
Water – 500ml

How it's done

1. Wash the lentils a couple of times to remove any dust and dirt. In a heavy-bottomed pan mix the dal with the water, salt, coriander powder, cumin powder, turmeric powder and bring to boil. Skim the top to remove any impurities and cook the lentils until soft, which takes approximately 20-25 minutes. Take off the heat and blitz the lentils with a blender until smooth.
2. Chop the coriander stems and slice the tomatoes.
3. Add the coriander stem and tomatoes to the lentils and bring back to boil. Simmer for another 10-15 minutes.
4. In the meantime, prep for the tempering.

Tempering

Oil – 25ml
Cumin seeds – 2gms
Curry leaves – 2gms
Ginger chopped – 6gms
Garlic chopped – 8gms
Green chilli chopped – 4gms

How it's done

1. In a separate pan heat the oil and add the cumin seeds. Allow them to pop and release their flavour to the oil. Now add the garlic and saute until it turns light brown. Add the ginger, green chilli and curry leaves. Stir for a minute and pour over the cooked lentils.
2. Take off the heat and cover it with a lid. Leave it for half an hour.
3. Pass the soup through a fine sieve.
4. Check the seasoning and serve hot with a splash of lemon juice.
5. Use a hand blender to make a foam.
6. Serve

CHICKEN PAKODA AND TOMATO RASAM

Chicken Pakoda

What you'll need

12 portions
Chicken supreme – 530gms (12 pcs)
Ginger chopped – 10gms
Green chilli chopped – 8gms
Curry leaves chopped – 4gms
Turmeric powder – 1gm
Crushed black peppercorns – 1gm
Salt – 5gms
Egg yolk – 1
Lemon juice – 10ml
Batter flour – 50gms (base recipe)
Water – 50ml

How it's done

1. Trim the chicken supreme and mix all of the ingredients together.
2. Deep fry it hot oil at 180C, fry for 3-4 minutes resting a minute in between.

Tomato Rasam

What you'll need

Portion 12 x 60ml
Tomatoes – 370gms (4pcs)
Kashmiri chilli powder – 4gms
Turmeric powder – 2gms
Salt – 10gms
Crushed black peppercorns – 2gms
Cumin powder – 2gms
Coriander powder – 2gms
Tamarind – 20gms
Jaggery – 30gms
Tomato puree – 150gms
Coriander leaf stems – 40gms
Water – 1.2 litre

How it's done

1. Blitz the tomatoes in a blender.
2. Chop the coriander stems.
3. Soak the tamarind in 100ml of lukewarm water for 10-15 minutes and pass through a sieve and keep the pulp, discard the seeds.
4. In a thick-bottomed pan place the blitzed tomato along with the Kashmiri chilli powder, turmeric powder, salt, chopped coriander stem, crushed black peppercorns, cumin powder, coriander powder, tamarind pulp, tomato puree, jaggery and water.
5. Bring to the boil and keep simmering for 30- 40 minutes.
6. Meanwhile prep for the tempering.

Tempering

What you'll need

Oil – 25ml
Garlic with skin on – 20gms
Mustard seeds – 2gms
Curry leaves – 2gms

How it's done

1. Slice the garlic with the skin on.
2. In a separate pan heat the oil and crackle the mustard seeds. Add the garlic and allow it turn golden brown. Then add the curry leaves and pour this over to the cooked tomato mixture.
3. Take off the heat and cover it with a lid. Leave it for half an hour.
4. Pass the soup through a fine sieve.
5. Check the seasoning and serve hot.

PIDIANDTHARAVU

Portion – 4. This duck is a classical Syrian Christian creation. It is Kottayam-style, with Pidi, which are steamed rice dumplings. They are poached in a spiced coconut sauce and topped with duck cooked with spices.

For the duck – method 1

Duck Breasts – 540gms (2pcs)
Green cardamon – 4 pods
Bay leaf – 2pcs
Cinnamon – 1pcs
Cloves – 4pcs
(The above spices are less than a gram each)

1. Remove the skin of the duck breast and cut each breast into 20-22 pieces.
2. In a pan place the duck skin along with the spices. Keep it on low heat, allowing the skin to render. It will take approximately 30 minutes to release all of the fat.

For the duck – method 2

Ginger chopped – 5gms
Green chilli chopped – 2gms
Coriander powder – 5gms
Crushed black peppercorns – 2gms
Turmeric powder – 2gms
Salt – 4gms
Curry leaves – 2gms
Lemon juice – 10ml
Water – 350ml

1. In a separate pan place the cubed duck breast along with the above ingredients.
2. Cook it on slow fire, till the duck breast is tender, which takes 20-25 approximately minutes.

For the duck – method 3

Onions sliced – 250gms
Ginger garlic paste – 10gms
Salt – 3gms
Crushed black peppercorns – 1gm
Fennel powder – 1gm
Garam masala powder – 1gm
Cardamom powder – 1gm

1. Sieve the duck fat into a separate pan and place it on the heat. Add the sliced onions and keep on stirring. Add the salt and cook the onions until the mixture becomes soft and starts to form a mash. Now add the ginger garlic paste and saute it for a minute.
2. Now add the stock water from the duck-breast-cooked-mixture little by little so that the onions becomes a mash.
3. Now add the cooked duck breast, stirring on a low heat.
4. Mix 30gms coconut milk powder with 100ml of lukewarm water
5. Now add the coconut milk into the cooked duck breast mixture and finally sprinkle the spices over the top.

Pidi (rice dumpling)

Rice flour – 100gms
Water – 120ml
Salt – 2gms

1. Dry roast the rice flour over a low heat for about two minutes. In another pan bring the water to boil and add salt.
2. Pour the boiling water into the roasted rice flour, little by little. Mix it over a low heat. Take out of the pan and knead into a dough. Leave aside to cool down for 10 minutes. Cover it with a wet cloth.
3. Knead it nicely and make 16 small dumpling weighing 8gms each. Cover the mixture with a wet cloth.
4. Boil 400ml of water. Place the dumplings into the hot water. Reduce the heat and allow the dumpling to cook for 8 to 10 minutes. Once cooked strain the dumplings and add to the coconut sauce.

Coconut Sauce

Coconut milk powder – 150gms
Water – 400ml
Salt – 6gms
Green chilli chopped – 2gms
Ginger chopped – 2gms
Cardamom powder – 2gms
Sugar – 4gms

1. Mix the coconut milk powder with 400ml of water and on a pan bring it to boil along with the green chilli, ginger, salt, sugar and cardamom powder. Simmer it for 10-15 minute until it reaches a sauce consistency. Now add the cooked rice dumpling and simmer for couple of minutes.

Tempering

Coconut oil – 20ml
Shallots sliced – 5gms
Curry leaves chopped – 2gms
Mustard seeds – 2gms

1. In a separate pan heat the oil and crackle the mustard seeds. Add the sliced shallots and saute until golden brown. Add the curry leaves. Pour the tempering into the coconut sauce.

Confit Duck Legs

Portion 4 – 25gms each
Confit duck legs (base recipe)

1. Preheat the oven to 180C and spread the pulled confit duck legs across a roasting tray. Roast for 4 minutes until the meat becomes crisp. Take it out of the oven.

To serve

1. Place the duck breast in the centre of a plate in a steel ring and arrange the four rice dumplings around the duck. Then pour the coconut sauce over and garnish with crispy duck leg confit and microcress.

CRAB

Crispy soft shell crab, crab cake and crab salad

Crab Cake

What you'll need

Portion – 6 x 30gms
White crab meat – 225gms
Chopped green chilli – 2gms
Chopped ginger – 10gms
Chopped red onions – 35gms
Chopped coriander leaves – 2gms
Salt – 3gms
Black pepper powder – 1gm

Lemon juice – 5ml
Egg yolk – 1
Oil – 10ml
Grated potato – 70ms (base recipe)
Eggs
Panko Japanese Breadcrumbs
Oil to fry

How it's done

1. Squeeze the crab meat to remove the excess water content.
2. Heat the oil in a pan, add ginger, green chilli and red onion and saute for a minute. Add the crab meat and stir it for couple of minutes.
3. Now add the black pepper powder, salt, coriander leaves and lemon juice.
4. Take it off the heat and mix it with egg yolk.
5. Allow the mixture to cool then mix with the grated potato and shape into balls weighing 30gms each.
6. Beat the eggs, dip the crab balls into the egg mixture and crumb it.
7. Fry it in hot oil.

Crab Salad

What you'll need

Portion 6
Crab claw meat – 180gms
Oil – 15ml
Poppy seeds – 2gms (Khus Khus)
Mustard seeds – 1gm
Garlic sliced – 5gms
Green chilli chopped – 2gms
Ginger chopped – 4gms
Onions chopped – 90gms

Salt – 2gms
Sweetcorn kernels – 30gms
Curry leaves – 2gms
Turmeric powder – 2gms
Madras curry powder – 2gms
Yoghurt – 50gms
Medium desiccated coconut – 40gms
Coconut milk powder – 40gms

How it's done

1. Squeeze the crab meat to remove any excess water content. Blend the coconut milk powder with 60ml of water.
2. Heat oil in pan and add poppy seeds and mustard seeds. Allow to pop then add the sliced garlic, chopped ginger, chopped green chilli, curry leaves and chopped onions. Saute for a couple of minutes, lower the heat and add turmeric powder, madras curry powder and salt.
3. Add the crab meat, yoghurt, desiccated coconut, sweetcorn kernels and coconut milk. Mix together and take off the heat.

Soft Shell Crab

What you'll need

Portion – 6
Soft shell crab – 6pcs
Curry leaf and garlic paste – 12gms (base recipe)
Batter flour – 60gms (base recipe)
Coriander leaves – 2gms
Turmeric powder – 1gm
Water – 60ml
Bell pepper sauce (base recipe)

How it's done

1. To clean the soft shell crab, remove the outer soft shell and throw away any dirt. Wash it nicely and keep on a colander to drain off the water.
2. Apply the curry leaf and garlic paste to the top of the soft shell crab.
3. Mix the batter flour with water and chopped coriander leaves and turmeric. Dip the marinated soft shell crab in the batter and carefully drop it into hot oil at a 200C. Fry it for minute until it becomes crisp.

To serve

1. Place the crab salad in a steel ring to retain its shape. Now add the soft shell crab and sit the crab cake on bell pepper sauce (base recipe), as in the photograph.

CHICKEN TIKKA CONNOISSEUR

What you'll need

Portion – 4
Chicken supreme – 4
Ginger garlic paste – 30gms
Mustard oil – 10ml
lemon juice – 12 ml
Salt – 6gms

How it's done

1. Trim the chicken supreme, remove the fat and and cut each supreme into 3 pieces, to make a total of 12 pieces from 4 supreme.
2. For the first marinade: place the 12 Chicken supreme pieces in a bowl and add ginger garlic paste, mustard oil, lemon juice and salt and keep it refrigerated for 1-2 hours.
3. Now we make three different marinades and divide the supreme into three bowls, each with four pieces of supreme. (See opposite)
4. Skewer the chicken and cook in a tandoor or in an oven by placing the chicken in a wire rack, preheating the oven to 250C and roasting for 5 minutes. Then baste it with melted butter and lower the temperature to 180C. Cook for another 5 minutes then sprinkle with chat masala and melted butter.

Malai (creamy cheese)

Green chilli – 2gms (chopped)
Ginger – 3gms (chopped)
Thyme – 1gm (chopped)
Philadelphia Cheese – 65gms (medium fat cheese)
Hung yoghurt – 20gms (base recipe)
Cardamom powder – 1gm
Single cream – 10ml

Mix all the ingredients together. Apply this marinade to the first marinated chicken supreme. Keep it for a couple of hours or even overnight.

Hara (basil)

Basil paste – 70gms (base recipe)
Hung yoghurt – 25gms
Coriander powder – 1gm
Cumin powder – 2gms
Rock salt – 2gms
Kasoori methi powder – 2gms
Black pepper powder – 2gms
Bhuno besan – 10gms (base recipe)

Mix all the ingredients together. Apply this marinade to the first marinated chicken supreme. Keep it for a couple of hours or even overnight.

Red chilli

Kashmiri chilli powder – 7gms
Hung yoghurt – 90gms
Ginger garlic paste – 8gms
Kasoori methi leaves – 1gm
Chat masala – 1gm
Amchur powder – 1gm
Chana masala powder – 1gm

Mix all the ingredients together. Apply this marinade to the first marinated chicken supreme. Keep it for a couple of hours or even overnight.

To serve

1. Pipe the mixed berry sauce (base recipe) and line the three tikkas malai, hara and red chilli as in the photograph.

STREETS OF MUMBAI

Potato Cake and Chana Masala

Portion – 6 pieces
Grated potato (base recipe) – 180gms
Roasted chana dal powder – 15gms
Melted butter – 10gms
Chat masala – 1gm

1. Mix the grated potatoes with roasted chana dal powder, butter and chat masala and form into a dough. Divide it into 30gms balls and shape them into a cake. Cook in a pan on both sides with butter until brown and crisp
2. Chana masala – 240gms (base recipe). Warm the chana masala in a pan and keep aside.
3. Now make remaining elements – see recipes opposite.

Bhel Puri

Portion – 6
Roasted puffed rice – 25gms. Dry roast in a pan to make it crisp and leave aside to cool down
Gram flour vermicelli – 48gms
Chopped red onions – 60gms
Tamarind chutney – 36gms (base recipe)
Mint sauce – 36gms (base recipe)

1. In a bowl mix all the above ingredients together.
2. Keep aside for plating, divide into six portions.

Bombay Chat

Portion – 6
Gol Gappa – 6 (semolina pastry)
Chick pea and potato mash (base recipe) – 24gms
Mint chutney (base recipe)
Tamarind chutney (base recipe)
Sweetened Yoghurt (base recipe)
Gram flour vermicelli
Pomegranate seeds

1. Make a small hole in the semolina pastry with the back of a spoon, add the chick pea and potato mash, approximately 4gms per pastry, top it with tamarind chutney 1gm, mint chutney 1gm, and fill up with sweetened yoghurt 8gms.
2. Garnish with gram flour vermicelli and pomegranate seeds.

To serve

1. Place the bhel puri in a steel ring, divide it into six portions at the top end of the plate, then add one quenelle of warm chana masala topped with crispy potato cakes. Now layer it with sweetened yoghurt in a piping bottle approximately (40gms) per portion so that it covers the chana masala and the potato cake. Then top with a drizzle of tamarind chutney, 8gms per portion, and keep the Bombay chat on the side.

FRESH FROM THE CREAMERY

Paneer Tikka – 4 portions

How it's done

1. Cut 230gms of paneer into four cubes weighing 55gms each
2. Now take: Water – 500ml; Turmeric powder- 1gm; Single cream- 25ml; Cardamom powder- 1gm; Salt- 3gms.
3. Pour the water into a pan with the turmeric powder, single cream, cardamom powder and salt. Blanch the paneer for a couple of minutes to make it soft, then drain in a colander.
4. Meanwhile, make the marinade.

Marinade

What you'll need

Ginger chopped – 4gms
Green chilli chopped – 2gms
Salt – 2gms
Philadelphia Cheese – 65gms (medium fat cheese)
Hung Yoghurt – 20gms
Honey – 30gms
Saffron – 1gm
Chopped coriander – 2gms

How it's done

1. Mix the ingredients in a bowl and place them around the paneer to marinade for an hour.
2. Pre heat the oven to 180 C and place the marinated paneer on a wire rack. Cook it for 8-10 minutes, baste it with melted butter then sprinkle it with chat masala.

Cheese Samosa

What you'll need

Portion – 4
Pear chutney – (base recipe)
Spring roll sheet – 4 pouches (base recipe)
Tintern cheese – 36gms
Mild cheddar cheese – 36gms
Cashew nut – 8gms (fry in hot oil until light golden brown)
Chopped green chilli – 2gms
Red onions chopped – 5gms
Chopped coriander leaves – 1gm
Plain flour
Oil to fry

How it's done

1. Grate the Tintern and the cheddar cheese into a bowl and mix with the fried cashew nuts, green chilli, onions and coriander leaves. Make a pouch with the spring roll sheet and fill it with the mixture.
2. Mix some flour with water to make a paste to stick the edges of the samosa together, which will stop the cheese mixture from oozing out.
3. Fry the samosa in hot oil at 180C for less than a minute.

Goat's Cheese and Pickled Beetroot Salad

What you'll need

Goat's cheese roundel – 4 pcs
Pickled beetroot – 12 slices (base recipe) 3 per portion
Spinach leaves – 12 (3 per portion)
Salad dressing (base recipe)
Bell pepper sauce (base recipe)
Tamarind chutney (base recipe)

How it's done

1. To serve blow torch the goat's cheese, to make it soft and warm.
2. Place the salad leaves on the plate. Drizzle the salad dressing and place the pickled beetroot above. Top it with goat's cheese.
3. On the middle of the plate, place one spoonful of pear chutney and let the samosa rest on it.
4. Add a drop of bell pepper sauce and place the cooked paneer on top of it. Garnish with microcress.

To serve

1. Plate as shown in photograph with tamarind chutney and bell pepper sauce.

CALAMARI

Portion – 4
Calamari – 4
Salt
Pepper
Batter flour – 50gms (base recipe)
Oil to fry

For Spice Powder (mix following ingredients together):
Kashmiri chilli powder – 6gms
Turmeric powder – 2gms
Crushed black peppercorns – 2gms
Chana masala powder – 2gms
Amchur powder – 2gms
Chat masala – 2gms
Fennel seed powder – 2gms
Salt – 2gms

How it's done

1. You'll need 4 medium sized squid cleaned and with quills and beaks removed.
2. Make five slits in between the tubes still holding the shape.
3. Sprinkle salt and crushed pepper on the squid.
4. Take batter flour – 50gms (base recipe).
5. Place the batter flour on a bowl and dust the squid tubes and fry it in hot oil. temperature of 200 C for 2-3 minutes till it's crisp and sprinkle the spice powder.
6. Make mixed salad (base recipe).
7. Make passion fruit and chilli dressing (base recipe).
8. On a pasta plate, place the salad and fried calamari with the spice crust and drizzle with passion fruit and chilli dressing.

LAMB

Seekh Kebab

What you'll need

Portion – 8
Lamb mince – 500gms
Ginger chopped – 15gms
Coriander leaves chopped – 10gms
Green chilli chopped – 2gms
Mint chopped – 2gms
Garlic chopped – 16gms
Kashmiri chilli powder – 10gms
Salt – 6gms

How it's done

1. Mix the lamb mince with the above ingredients, and divide into 8 portions of 60gms. Roll into balls.
2. Wet your hands and using your fingers, slowly spread the mince on the skewers to make kebabs that are 10cm long. To avoid the mixture sticking, keep your hand wet and intermittently run water over the kebabs as you make them. This will smooth the outer texture of the kebab and make sure the kebabs are quite thick, which helps to retain their flavour and juices.
3. Cook the kebab on the tandoor or under a grill or barbeque at 250C for 6-8 minutes, turning regularly to ensure the meat is cooked evenly.

Lamb Pattice

What you'll need

Portion – 16 x 30gms each
Oil – 25ml
Lamb mince – 300gms
Garlic chopped– 10gms
Green chilli chopped – 2gms
Ginger chopped – 2gms
Chopped onions – 175gms
Ginger garlic paste – 12gms
Salt – 6gms
Turmeric powder – 2gms
Kashmiri chilli powder – 4gms

Coriander powder – 6gms
Tomatoes chopped – 40gms
Water – 350ml
Coriander leaves, chopped – 2gms
Garam masala powder – 1gm

Grated Potatoes - 200gms
Eggs
Breadcrumbs
Oil to fry

How it's done

1. Heat oil in a thick bottomed pan. Add chopped garlic and allow to turn golden brown. Then add chopped ginger, green chilli and the chopped onions and cook for a further 12-15 minutes until the onions turns light brown.
2. Add the lamb mince and sauté for a couple of minutes. Now add the ginger garlic paste and cook until the raw smells disappear and the mixture starts catching the bottom of the pan. Now lower the heat add the turmeric powder, coriander powder, Kashmiri chilli powder, salt and stir for a minute without burning the spices.
3. Add the chopped tomatoes and cook further. Add 200ml water, bringing it to boil. Cover with a lid and simmer for 10-12 minutes.
4. Check the lamb and add the remaining 150ml of water. Once the lamb mince is cooked, sprinkle it with chopped coriander leaves and garam masala powder. Allow the mixture to cool.
5. Mix the grated potatoes with cooked lamb mixture, shape into ball weighing 30gms each.
6. Keep in the fridge for half an hour to maintain their shape. Dip it the beaten eggs, crumb it and deep fry 180C for two minutes. Rest and serve hot.

Keema Pao with Quail Eggs

What you'll need

Portion – 16 portion of 25gms
Oil – 40ml
Lamb mince – 300gms
Fennel seeds – 2gms
Onions sliced – 300gms
Salt – 4gms
Crushed black peppercorns – 2gms
Turmeric powder – 2gms
Kashmiri chilli powder – 2gms

Coriander powder – 3gms
Ginger garlic paste – 12gms
Fennel powder – 2gms
Tomato puree – 30gms
Water – 400ml
Pao/Brioche – 16 (base recipe)
16 quail eggs
Melted butter

How it's done

1. Heat oil in a thick-bottomed pan. Add the sliced onion and cook for 15 minutes until light golden brown.
2. Now add the lamb mince and fennel seeds and braise for a further 3- 4 minutes. Add the ginger garlic paste and cook until the raw smells disappear and the mix starts catching. Now lower the heat, add turmeric powder, Kashmiri chilli powder, coriander powder, salt and stir for a minute without burning the spices. Then add tomato puree.
3. Add the water with 200ml initially. Bring to the boil and cover with a lid. Simmer for 10-12 minutes.
4. Check the lamb and add another 200ml of water. Simmer for another 10 minutes.
5. Once the lamb mince is cooked, sprinkle with fennel powder and crushed black peppercorns. Allow to cool.
6. Divide the mixture into 25gm and add one quail egg per portion.
7. In a pan, fry the quail eggs. Keep the sunny side up. Cut the top of the brioche and brush it with melted butter and toast it in a pan. Place the lamb mince on the brioche and top it with a quail egg.

To serve

1. Put a drop of bell pepper sauce on the plate and place the lamb pattice on top of it followed by the seekh kebab and brioche.

PRAWNS

Malabar Prawns

What you'll need

Portion – 12 x 40gms
Kodumpuli (coccum) – 10gms
Shrimps – 640gms
Tamarind – 30gms
Water – 400ml

Coconut oil – 50ml
Mustard seeds – 4gms
Salt – 8gms
Turmeric powder – 4gms
Kashmiri chilli powder – 15gms
Asafoetida (hing) – 2gms
Ginger chopped – 10gms
Coconut chopped – 25gms
Curry leaves chopped – 4gms

What you'll need

1. In a separate pan, boil the tamarind and coccum then simmer for 15-20 minutes to get a tangy water. Strain, keep the water and discard the rest.
2. In a separate pan, heat the oil and crackle the mustard seeds. Add the ginger and coconut then lower the heat. Add the turmeric powder, Kashmiri chilli powder, hing, curry leaves and the strained tangy water along with the salt. Bring it to the boil. Now add the shrimps and boil for two minutes. Take off the heat and leave them in the sauce for at least one hour, so that they absorb all the flavours.
3. In separate non-stick pan, add the shrimps along with the sauce. Stir fry on a high heat for 10-12 minutes until all the sauce evaporates and the shrimps get a nice coating from the masala. Check the seasoning and serve hot. Serve in small wooden boats.

Prawn Samosa

What you'll need

Portion– 12 pieces
Prawns 16/20- 270gms (shell removed and chopped)
Oil – 20ml
Coriander seeds crushed – 2gms
Fennel seeds – 2gms
Salt – 2gms
Coriander leaves chopped – 5gms
Ginger chopped – 8gms
Green chilli chopped– 4gms
Spring roll sheet – 12 pouches (base recipe)
Plain flour
Oil to fry

How it's done

1. Heat the oil in a pan and add ginger and green chilli followed by chopped prawns. Saute for a minute and add salt, crushed coriander seeds, crushed fennel seeds and chopped coriander. Take off the heat and allow to cool down.
2. Divide the mixture into 20gms per samosa, which will give 12 samosa.
3. Make a pouch with the spring roll sheet.
4. Mix some flour with water to make a paste to stick the edges of the samosa together, which will stop the mixture from oozing out when frying. Fill the pouch with the prawn mixture. Fry the samosa in hot oil at 180C for a minute.

Tandoori King Prawn

What you'll need

Portion – 12
King prawn – 12 piece (6-8 size)

For Mustard paste:
Oil – 10ml
Green chilli chopped – 2gms
Ginger chopped – 5gms
Wholegrain mustard – 30gms
English mustard – 20gms
Turmeric powder – 1gm
Salt – 1gm

Second set of ingredients:
Ginger chopped – 1gm
Green chilli chopped – 1gm
Hung yoghurt – 25gms
Salt – 1gm
Chopped coriander leaves – 2gms

How it's done

1. Clean and de-vein prawns and slit from centre to the bottom.
2. Heat the oil in a pan. Add ginger and green chilli and stir for a minute. Add the wholegrain mustard and mustard paste, turmeric, salt and cook on a low heat for 8-10 minutes. Allow to cool down. In a separate bowl mix the cooked mustard paste with the second set of ingredients and the king prawns.
3. Preheat the oven to 180C and cook the prawns for 4-6 minutes.

To serve

1. Serve the Malabar prawns in a boat, prawn samosa on top pear chutney (base recipe), and tandoori king prawns on the side.

SALMON

Tandoori Salmon

What you'll need

Portion – 12
First marinade:
Salmon Tikka – 840gms (70gms x 12)
Ginger garlic paste – 15gms
Salt – 3gms
Fresh dill leaves chopped – 1gm

Second marinade:
Hung yoghurt – 60gms
Single cream – 40ml
Philadelphia cheese, mild – 120gms
Ginger chopped – 6gms
Green chilli chopped – 3gms
Salt – 1gm
Honey – 40gms

How it's done

1. Take a salmon fillet that has been pin-boned and scaled. It should weigh 1.7-1.8kg. Divide the salmon into three parts. Use the chunkiest part for the tikka and cut each portion into 65-70gms, making a total of 12 portions (830-850gms). Leave 500gms for the salmon pickle and the remainder for the cake.
2. Leave the salmon in the first marination for half-an-hour. Meanwhile make the second marinade in a separate bowl.
3. Gently mix the marinade with a whisk. Slowly combine. Pour onto the first-marinaded salmon tikka. Leave for at least an hour.

Salmon Pickle

What you'll need

Portion – 12
First set of ingredients:
Vegetable oil – 15ml
Ginger garlic paste – 30gms
Lemon juice – 20ml
Salt – 5gms
Kashmiri chilli powder – 7gms
Turmeric powder – 2gms
Oil to fry

Second set of ingredients:
Vegetable oil – 150ml
Fenugreek seeds – 2gms

Mustard seeds – 2gms
Ginger julienne – 20gms
Garlic sliced – 40gms
Green chilly sliced – 10gms
Curry leaves – 2gms
Kashmiri chilli powder – 20gms
Turmeric powder – 2gms
Asafoetida – 3gms
Salt – 2gms
Vinegar – 150ml
Sugar – 2gms

How it's done

1. Cut each piece of salmon into 10gms to make a total of 50 pieces. Place the salmon cubes in a bowl and mix with the first set of ingredients.
2. Deep fry the salmon cubes at 150C for a couple of minutes and keep aside.
3. Now using the second set of ingredients, heat the oil in a pan.
4. Place the fenugreek seeds in a low heat and allow them to turn dark brown so that they give a very good aroma. Turn the heat up then add the mustard seeds and allow them to crackle. Add the sliced garlic and cook until golden brown. Add the ginger julienne, sliced green chilli and curry leaves and saute for another two minutes.
5. Lower the heat and add the Kashmiri chilli powder, turmeric powder, salt, asafoetida and vinegar and bring back to the heat. Add the sugar, check the seasoning and add the fried salmon cubes to the pan.
6. Boil and then remove from the heat. Allow to cool down. Store in an air tight container and serve at room temperature.

Salmon cake

Portion – 18 pieces x 35gms
Vegetable oil – 25ml
Mustard seeds – 2gms
Garlic chopped – 8gms
Ginger chopped – 8gms
Green chilli chopped – 2gms
Curry leaves chopped – 2gms
Leek chopped – 30gms
Celery chopped – 40gms
Turmeric powder – 2gms
Coriander powder – 3gms

Madras curry powder – 4gms
Crushed black peppercorns – 2gms
Salt – 5gms
Grated potatoes – 250gms (base recipe)
Eggs
Breadcrumbs
Oil to fry

How it's done

1. Use all the leftover trimmings from the salmon tikka and pickle.
2. Steam the salmon trimmings in a small steamer, for 8-10 minutes so that they are still pink and juicy. Meanwhile make the masala for the cake.
3. Heat the oil in a pan. Add the mustard seeds and allow them to crackle. Add the chopped garlic and allow it to turn golden. Add the chopped ginger, chopped green chilli, chopped curry leaves and sauté for a minute. Add the chopped leeks and celery and stir while cooking for a couple of minutes. Lower the heat and add the turmeric powder, coriander powder, madras curry powder, salt and crushed black peppercorns. Now place the steamed salmon and mix. Take off the heat and allow it to cool.
4. Once cooled, mix with grated potatoes. Check the seasoning if needed. Weigh each cake into 35gms balls. Shape like a cake in your hands. Dip it in beaten eggs, crumb and deep fry at 180C.
5. Preheat the oven to 200C and cook the salmon tikka for 3 minutes. Lower the temperature to 180C and cook for another 2-3 minutes.

To serve

1. To plate, spoon the salmon pickle in 4 pieces per portion, with a salmon cake on the side with mint sauce, followed by tandoori salmon and tamarind chutney.

KAPPAMEEN

Kappa

What you'll need

Portion – 4
For tapioca mash:
Tapioca – 300gms (skin removed and cut into small cubes)
Kashmiri chilli powder – 2gms
Turmeric powder – 1gm
Salt – 6gms
Water – 400ml
Coconut oil – 10ml

Grated coconut – 40gms
Madras onions/Shallots – 30gms
Ginger – 2gms
Garlic – 6gms
Kashmiri whole chilli – 3gms

Tempering:
Curry leaves – 2gms
Coconut oil – 40ml
Mustard seeds – 2gms

How it's done

1. In a pan, place the tapioca and Kashmiri chilli powder, salt, turmeric powder, coconut oil (10ml) and water. Boil until the tapioca is cooked, which will take a good 25-30 minutes. With the back of the spoon, mash the tapioca in the pan.
2. Deseed the whole red chilly, crush garlic, ginger, followed by red chilli and shallots in a mortar and pestle until coarse, keep aside, coarse grind the grated coconut.
3. Heat the coconut oil and add the mustard seeds. Allow them to crackle. Add the crushed garlic, ginger, red chilli, curry leaves and shallots and saute for a minute. Add the coarse ground coconut and sauté for another 2-3 minutes. Add the cooked tapioca and mix it well so that it has a mashed texture. Check the seasoning and keep aside. The yield of tapioca mash will be 480gms.

Roasted Coconut Sauce

What you'll need

Portion – 4
Desiccated coconut fine – 50gms
Ginger sliced – 6gms
Garlic sliced – 8gms
Green chilli – 1gm
Curry leaves – 1gm
Kashmiri whole chilli – 2gms
Fenugreek seeds-6 pieces (less than half a gram)
Kashmiri chilli powder – 2gms
Coriander powder – 8gms
Turmeric powder – 1gm

Tamarind – 20gms
Kodumpuli – 15gms (coccum)

Coconut milk powder – 40gms
Blend coconut milk powder with 100ml of water
Coconut oil – 25ml
Chatpata sauce – 80gms (base recipe)
Salt – 4gms

How it's done

1. Dry roast the first set of ingredients in a pan for 10 minutes and grind to a fine paste with 300ml of water.
2. In a separate pan place the tamarind and kodumpuli with 300ml of water. Simmer for 10-15 minutes. Strain through a sieve, keep the pulp and discard the rest.
3. Heat the coconut oil and add the chatpata sauce. Sauté for a minute. Now add the roasted coconut paste, tamarind and coccum pulp, coconut milk and salt. Bring it to the boil and simmer the sauce for another 20-25 minutes. Strain the sauce through a sieve and keep aside, the yield of the sauce will be 440gms.

Hake

What you'll need

Portion – 4
Hake fillet – 450-480gms (descale, pin bone and trim the fillets)
Rock salt – 5gms

How it's done

1. On a tray, place the hake fillets. Sprinkle the rock salt on the flesh side of the fillet and keep in a refrigerator for at least an hour.
2. Wash the fillets in running cold water. Pat dry with a cloth and wrap it tight with cling film. Keep in the refrigerator for an hour. This will make the fillet firm and create a good shape when you slice the individual portion.

To serve

Oil
Butter
Ulli chutney (base recipe)

1. Portion the hake fillets into four, approximately 100-110gms per portion. Divide the tapioca mash into four, 100-110 gms per portion. Reheat the roasted coconut sauce
2. Heat the pan and add the oil. Place the hake fillets skin side down into the pan and cook on a medium heat for 4-5 minutes. Add the butter to the pan and baste the fillets with butter with a spoon. Turn the fillets. The skin should be crisp. Cook the other side for another 2-3 minutes.
3. To plate: place the tapioca mash in the centre with a steel ring, pour the roasted coconut sauce around it, allowing 100-110gms per portion. Place the hake fillets skin side up and apply the ulli chutney on the top. Serve hot.

Four ladies
and one chef

Some of the biggest influences on my life and cooking have been four ladies and one chef including my mother Philomena George (pictured below). In this section of the book I wanted to tell you something about each of them and share one of their recipes with you.

My mother Philomena George

My mother fed me with love and affection. She transformed my perception and understanding of food. Right from my childhood I remember the aroma and fragrance from her kitchen, where I used to sit and do my homework for school.

My mother's culinary repertoire was enhanced by my father's desire to eat a variety of meals. Pushed by my father, my mother created new recipes and dishes for us to try and experience.

Birthdays and festivals were celebrated with great meals at home. One of my favourites from her cooking was Ellam Kappa, where tapioca and beef brisket were cooked together with aromatic spices.

She dedicated her entire time to our family and stood very firm with me right from the beginning so that we understood her principles. She simply wanted us to be good human beings.

She passed the legacy of cooking food with love and affection to me. She gave me a grounding in great food, handing me the recipes she used to cook for us when I ventured into the culinary world to become a chef.

My mother still lives in Kochi with her partner, Chaliyachan Dominic Milton. She cooks me my favourite dishes whenever I return to see her.

I have recreated a dish from her cooking that features a braised egg and is eaten with idiyappam (string hoppers). See Pages 102 - 103

My friend's mother Shyama Nair

I eventually found my way into a professional kitchen and that was in no small part down to my aunty, a lady called Shyama Nair.

Shyama was the mother of my friend, Krishna Kumar. I'd become very close with his family during my last years at college in Kochi.

Krishna was a housekeeper at a hotel in Rajasthan and later he moved to Dubai. I became a big part of their family then became very close to Shyama aunty who helped me to realise my dream of becoming a chef. I loved eating aunty's vegetarian dishes and my favourite was appam – rice pancake with vegetables stewed with aromatic spices and coconut milk.

Eating meals at aunty's place gave me an insight and understanding of the culinary practices of the Nair community of Kerala. It helped me to learn their culture and traditions. It also encouraged me to use local produce to create exotic dishes. The classic Kerala Sadhya, a lavish lunch with 18 dishes on a banana leaf, is still my favorite. I am sharing the recipe for vegetable stew that I learned from her.

See Pages 106 - 107

My mother's sister Rosily aunty

Rosily aunty was a real foodie and I enjoyed listening to her stories.

She had great charisma in narrating tales and I used to visit her during the school holidays when she would cook a feast for us.

She learned cooking from our great grandmother and used to give us a lots of goodies, like Achappam (rose cookies) and Avolos unda.

Going to the market with her was fun and the way she liaised with fishmongers and street vendors to get a bargain was very interesting.

Rosily aunty and Antony uncle were food lovers.

They cooked with real passion and enthusiasm. One of the greatest dishes I admired from her cooking was beef cooked with cabbage, a humble dish that transformed simple ingredients into a great meal.

I have recreated that recipe from my memories.

See Pages 104 - 105

My dad's sister Pushpy aunty

Pushpy aunty married Thomas Jacob, of Athiyalil House, Ponkunnam, Kottayam, Kerala.

During our school holidays we visited our grandmother's place in Kuttanad.

Pushpy aunty visited there too with her kids and at other times she visited us in Kochi.

Pushpy aunty cooked food with great care and affection and her culinary expertise showcased the Syrian Christian style of cooking; that was my father's heritage.

The exposure I had of eating tasty food inspired me to create new dishes.

One of my favourites of Pushpy aunty's cooking was a Kuttanad-style Duck Roast, where the whole duck was cubed with the skin on and braised with aromatic spices and herbs.

My tongue still tingles when I think about that dish.

Pushpy aunty, like the other ladies and chef, inspired me throughout my journey by sharing the rich heritage of Keralan food and hospitality.

See Pages 108 - 109

William – an inspiring chef from Kochi

Kuttathil Parambu Antony Wilfred (Willy) is a great chef from the old school.

He learned his culinary art from working in the bungalows of families that had an Anglo- Indian connection.

Those families had big businesses and would entertain guests at home.

They would train their chefs to cook meals for their clients.

Chef Willy had a great opportunity because he worked in several such houses where he would be supervised by the lady of the house.

I was introduced to Chef Willy through a mutual friend when I was researching Anglo Indian recipes.

I was truly inspired by Chef Willy's cooking. His eye for detail with spices and flavourings inspired me and I still respect his skills and am grateful that he has shared recipes with me.

When I think of Chef Willy's cooking, the dish that strikes me was his green fish curry. I have tried my level best to recreate that recipe with a subtle twist. I sincerely thank Chef William for his kind heart in sharing his recipes and experiences: Through him I have learned dishes from the old time. He is presently the Chef at the Secret Garden, a boutique homestay in Fort Kochi.

See Pages 110 - 111

BRAISEDEGG –
MOM

What you'll need

Portion – 5
Tomatoes – 200gms
Coriander powder – 20gms
Turmeric powder – 2gms
Kashmiri chilli powder – 8gms
Ginger – 22gms
Garlic – 30gms
Curry leaves – 3gms
Green chilli – 10gms
Oil – 50ml

Salt – 14gms
Water – 1 litre
Coconut milk powder – 100gms (blended with 300 ml of water and kept aside)

Tempering
Oil – 25ml
Madras onions, or shallots – 60gms sliced
Curry leaves – 2gms

Eggs – 10 (5 portions)

How it's done

1. Slice the onions, garlic and tomatoes, slit the green chilli and julienne the ginger.
2. Heat the oil in a thick-bottomed pan and add the garlic, ginger, green chilli and curry leaves. Sauté for a minute, then add the onions and keep stirring for another 20-25 minutes.
3. Now lower the heat and add the coriander powder, Kashmiri chilli powder, turmeric powder, salt and tomatoes. Keep sautéing for a further 8-10 minutes until the tomatoes mash. Now add the water and bring it to boil. Keep simmering for another 8-10 minutes. Now add the coconut milk and bring it to the boil again. Simmer until it reaches a sauce consistency, which should take 8-10 minutes.
4. Meanwhile make a tempering: In a separate pan, heat the oil and cook the shallots until golden brown. Then add the curry leaves and pour the tempering over the simmering sauce. Check the seasoning and take off the heat.
5. Preheat the oven 180C
6. In a separate non-stick pan, place 300gms of the sauce. Crack the eggs into two separate ramekins and pour the eggs from the ramekins into the non-stick pan. Place into the oven and braise for 6-7 minutes, depending on how runny a yolk you prefer. Serve with idiyappam (string hoppers).

BEEFANDCABBAGE – ROSILYAUNTY

What you'll need

Portion – 4
Beef flank boneless – 1140gms
Cabbage white – 450gms
Coconut oil/Vegetable oil – 50ml
Onions sliced – 400gms
Green chilly slit – 10gms
Curry leaves – 4gms
Ginger julienne – 20gms
Tomatoes sliced – 150gms
Kashmiri chilli powder – 4gms
Turmeric powder – 2gms
Water – 1.2 litre
Salt – 12gms

Spice powder
Black Peppercorns – 8gms
Cloves – 1gm
Cinnamon – 2gms

How it's done

1. Trim the beef flank and cut into small cubes each weighing 35-40gms.
2. Remove the damaged leaves of the cabbage, remove the core and cut into big cubes.
3. In a blender, powder black peppercorns, cloves, cinnamon and keep aside. Heat coconut oil in a heavy-bottomed pan and add onions, ginger, green chilli, curry leaves and saute for 8-10 minutes.
4. Once the onions are soft, lower the heat and add Kashmiri chilli powder, turmeric powder, the spice powder, beef cubes, salt and tomatoes. Stir for a couple of minutes.
5. Add water and bring to boil. Cook on a low heat with a lid on for another two hours, stirring occasionally. Make sure the masala doesn't burn and if it needs more moisture add additional water. Once the beef flank is cooked and the sauce is reduced, add the cubed cabbage leaves and stir fry for 4-5 minutes.
6. Don't cook the cabbage too long. It should keep its bite. Check the seasoning and serve hot.

VEGETABLESTEW – SHYAMAAUNTY

What you'll need

Portion – 6
Cauliflower florets – 90gms
Carrots – 130gms
French beans – 100gms
Broccoli florets – 90gms
Potatoes – 350gms

Vegetable oil/ coconut oil – 50ml
Onions sliced – 300gms
Ginger julienne – 20gms
Green chilli slit – 15gms
Curry leaves – 2gms
Salt – 12gms

Peppercorns – 2gms
Cloves – 1gm
Cinnamon – 4gms
Green cardamom – 2gms
Water – 1litre
Coconut milk powder – 100gms

Tempering
Pure butter ghee/oil – 50gms
Mustard seeds – 2gms
Curry leaves – 2gms
Madras onions sliced(shallots) – 50gms
Golden raisins – 30gms

How it's done

1. Peel the potatoes and carrots then cut into small cubes. String the beans and cut each into two. Blend the coconut milk powder with 300ml of water and keep aside.
2. In a thick-bottomed pan, heat the coconut oil and add the peppercorns, cinnamon, cloves and cardamom followed by the ginger, green chilli, curry leaves and onions. Sauté for a minute without browning.
3. Add water along with salt and bring to the boil. Let the water reduce for another 15minutes so that the onions become translucent and soft. Add the cubed potatoes and cook for 6-7 minutes followed by the carrots and cauliflower and cook for another 3-4 minutes.
4. Now add the French beans and cook for another 2 minutes. Finally add the broccoli and the coconut milk. Cook for another 2-3 minutes. Make sure the vegetables are not over-cooked and still have bite.
5. In a separate pan heat the butter ghee. Add the mustard seeds and allow them to pop.
6. Next, add the shallots and cook for another 2-3 minutes, stirring in between. When they start to brown add the raisins and saute until golden brown. Add the curry leaves. Pour the tempering into the vegetable stew. Check the consistency of the sauce and the seasoning and serve hot.

NADANTHARAVUROAST – PUSHPYAUNTY

What you'll need

Portions – 5
Whole duck – 2.3kg
Cinnamon stick – 2gms
Green cardamom – 2gms
Cloves – 1gm
Bay leaf – 2gms

Madras curry powder – 20gms
Coriander powder – 20gms
Turmeric powder – 10gms
Kashmiri chilli powder – 15gms
Salt – 18gms

Onion sliced – 1650gms
Tomatoes sliced – 300gms
Ginger julienne – 70gms
Curry leaves – 10gms

How it's done

1. Remove the skin from the whole duck and cut into small pieces with bone on. There should be about 28- 30 pieces. Place the skin on a thick-bottomed pan along with cinnamon stick, green cardamom, cloves and bay leaf and render the fat.
2. Keep it on a medium heat for 15 minutes until the fat melts from the skin. Discard the skin and sieve the melted fat into a thick-bottomed pan, which will give you a flavoured oil. Bring back to a low heat and add the second set of powdered spices.
3. Stir it on a low heat without burning for a couple of minutes.
4. Now add the sliced onions and ginger julienne to the pan with the powdered spices. Keep stirring for 30-40 minutes. Once the onions become mashed, add the sliced tomatoes. Cook for another 10 minutes. Now add the cubed duck pieces and braise with onion masala. Cook on a medium flame for 45- 50 minutes, stirring in between and covering with a lid. Now add 400 ml of water and cook for another 30-40 minutes. Keep the lid on and stir occasionally until the duck is cooked.

Tempering

Vegetable oil/ coconut oil – 50ml
Garlic sliced – 50gms
Crushed black peppercorns – 4gms
Garam masala powder – 4gms
Fennel powder – 2gms

1. Slice the garlic thinly and heat the oil in a separate pan. Cook the garlic until golden brown. Add the black peppercorns, garam masala powder and fennel powder and pour the tempering on the cooked duck. Check the seasoning and serve hot.

GREEN FISH CURRY – CHEF WILLIAM

What you'll need

Portion – 4

For Green paste:
Ginger – 10gms
Garlic – 20gms
Green chilli – 10gms
Coriander leaves – 53gms
Bell pepper, green – 1 piece
Lemon juice – 10ml

Green sauce:
Onions sliced – 200gms
Cashew nuts – 50gms
Water – 300ml

Oil – 25ml
Salt – 6gms
Crushed black peppercorns – 2gms
Turmeric powder – 2gms
Lemon juice – 10ml
Water – 200ml

Sea bream whole – 4
Turmeric powder – 8gms
Salt – 8gms
Crushed pepper – 8gms
Oil – 40ml
Lemon juice – 40ml

How it's done

1. Boil the onions and cashew nuts in the 300ml of water for approximately 30 minutes. Remove from the heat and blend to a fine paste. Set aside.
2. De-seed the bell pepper, removing the core and the white membrane. Roughly chop.
3. In a blender add the ginger, garlic, green chilli, coriander leaves, green pepper, lemon juice and grind to a fine paste. Keep aside.
4. In a separate pan, heat the oil and add the boiled onion and cashew paste. Cook on a low heat for 10-12 minutes. Add the turmeric powder, salt and water and bring back to the boil. Once the sauce thickens add the green paste. Bring to the boil and quickly finish with lemon juice and crushed black peppercorns. Take off the heat and pass through a strainer. Portion into ramekins for service.
5. Meanwhile make a marinade for the fish with salt, crushed peppercorns, oil, turmeric powder, lemon juice.
6. Remove the scales, and head of the fish, make gashes on both sides of the fish and marinade.
7. Pre heat the oven to 240C and cook the whole fish for 8-10 minutes, or alternatively pan fry it.
8. Serve the cooked fish with the green sauce on the side.

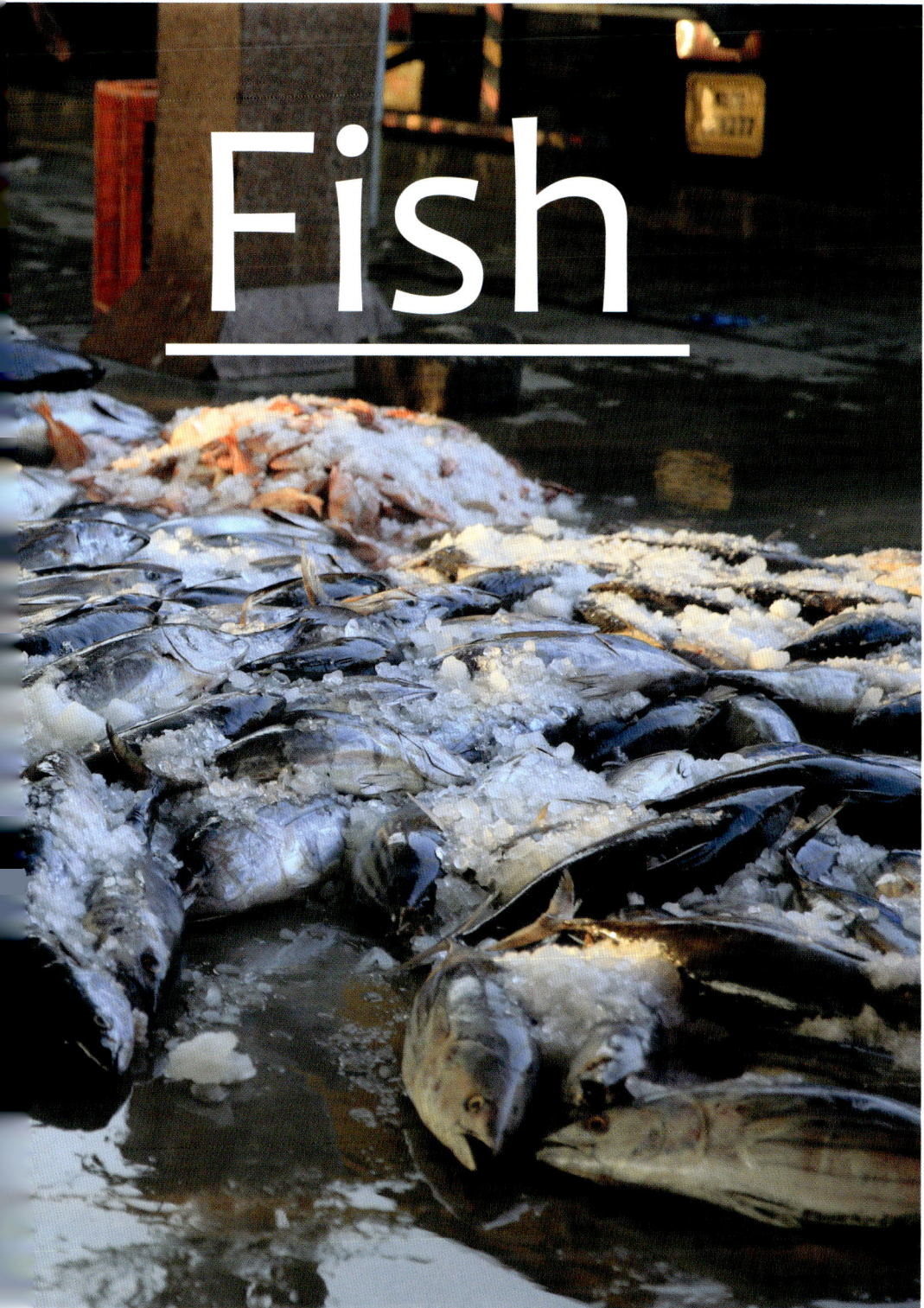

Fish

TIFFIN SEABASS

This signature dish commemorates my victory in the House of Commons Tiffin Cup in 2008. It comprises seabass fillets pan seared and served on a bed of curry leaf-infused mashed potato with a raw mango, ginger and coconut sauce.

Alleppey Sauce

What you'll need

Portion – 6
Oil – 25 ml
Onions – 150gms
Raw mango – 150gms (three small mangoes, firm and sour with the skin removed, deseeded and chopped)

Ginger – 10gms
Curry Leaf – 5gms
Kashmiri chilli powder – 15gms
Turmeric powder – 10gms
Maggi coconut milk powder – 300gms
Salt – 12gms
Water – 900ml

How it's done

1. Peel and slice the onions, julienne the ginger and peel the raw mango then cut it into small cubes.
2. Mix the coconut milk powder with 600ml of hot water and blend it well.
3. Heat the oil in a pan, add the sliced onions, ginger, raw mango and curry leaves. Sauté until it becomes transparent.
4. Lower the flame then add the Kashmiri chilli powder, turmeric powder and salt, sauté for couple of minutes and then add 300 ml of water and bring it to boil, simmer it for some more time, then add 600ml of water and simmer it for another 15 minutes. When the mixture starts thickening add the coconut milk and cook until the sauce consistency is smooth. It will take a good half hour of simmering. Take off the heat and pass through a fine sieve. Check the seasoning.

Curry Leaf Mash Potato

Potatoes grated – 600gms (base recipe)
Oil – 30 ml
Mustard seeds – 5gms
Split urad dal – 10gms
Onions – 150gms
Ginger – 10gms
Green chilli – 5gms
Curry leaves – 3gms
Salt – 6gms
Turmeric powder – 2gms
Water – 50ml

1. Chop the onions, green chilli, ginger and curry leaf.
2. Heat the oil in a pan, add split urad dal and allow it to turn into golden brown. Add the mustard seeds and allow to crackle to release their flavour. Add the chopped ginger, onion, green chilli and curry leaf.
3. Lower the heat. Add the turmeric powder and salt then sauté for a minute. Add the water, the grated potatoes and mash well. Check seasoning. Divide the mash into six portions.

To cook the fish

6 pieces of sea bass fillets
Sea salt to sprinkle on fish
Butter

1. Cut each sea bass fillet into two.
2. Sprinkle the sea salt on sea bass fillets and brush a bit of butter on the skin side. Heat the pan, place the bass fillets skin-side down and cook both sides (approximately 2- 3 minutes).
3. Pour the Alleppey sauce onto the plate. Place the curry leaf mashed potato on the centre of the sauce and finally rest the cooked bass fillets on top.
4. Garnish with beetroot pachadi and fried curry leaf.
5. Serve as in photograph with beetroot pachadi (base recipe).

SEABASSPOLLICHATHU

What you'll need

Portion – 4
Sea Bass fillets – 4 pcs (150-180gms each)
Coconut oil/ vegetable oil – 60ml
Mustard seeds – 2gms
Ginger chopped – 20gms
Garlic chopped – 20gms
Green chilli chopped – 5gms
Red onions chopped – 150gms
Madras onions/ shallots, sliced – 150gms
Curry leaves chopped – 2gms
Salt – 8gms
Kashmiri chilli powder – 8gms
Turmeric powder – 2gms
Coriander powder – 6gms

Tomato chopped – 175gms
Tomato paste – 30gms
Kodumpuli/coccum – 30gms
Tamarind – 20gms

Marinate the sea bass fillets with:
Lemon juice – 20ml
Vegetable oil – 20ml
Salt – 8gms
Kashmiri chilli powder – 6gms
Turmeric powder – 2gms
You will also need Banana leaf/
parchment paper – 4

How it's done

1. Place the coccum and tamarind in a pan with 150ml of water. Bring it to the boil and simmer for 15-20 minutes. Pass it through a strainer, keeping the pulp and discarding the rest.
2. Heat the oil in a pan. Add the mustard seeds and allow them to crackle. Add the garlic, ginger, green chilli and curry leaves. Sauté until they turn golden brown. Add the red onions and shallot and cook for another 7-8 minutes. Lower the heat and add the Kashmiri chilli powder, turmeric powder and coriander powder. Stir for a minute. Now add the chopped tomato, tomato paste and salt. Once the tomatoes soften add the pulp from tamarind and coccum. Cook for another 6-7 minutes until a thick onion tomato masala is formed, rather than a paste. Check the seasoning and keep aside.
3. Cut the banana leaf into a piece large enough to hold each fillet. Wipe the banana leaf with a wet cloth to remove dust and any dirt. Place the leaves on the heat for a couple of seconds to make it pliable.
4. Divide the cooked masala into 4 portions, approximately 100-110gms per portion.
5. On the banana leaf keep the half of the masala then the sea bass fillets followed by the other half of the masala. Wrap nicely like a book fold so that no juices or steam can escape in cooking. The banana leaf gives a unique flavour but if it is not available you can use parchment paper instead.
6. Preheat the oven to 180C and cook the wrapped fillets for 8 minutes. Alternatively you can cook in a pan, by cooking both sides for 3-4 minutes each side.

BOATMAN FISH CURRY

What you'll need

Portion – 4

Monkfish fillets – 700-800gms (cleaned and cut into 50gms X 12 pieces)
Coconut oil – 75ml
Mustard seeds – 2gms
Fenugreek seeds – 2gms
Madras onions/shallots – 150gms (or use shallots)
Garlic – 50gms
Ginger – 30gms
Curry leaves – 2gms
Salt – 12gms
Tomato paste – 50gms
Turmeric powder – 5gms
Kashmiri chilli powder – 25gms
Water – 400ml
Kodumpuli/coccum – 50gms
Tamarind – 20gms

How it's done

1. Place the tamarind and Kodumpuli/coccum in a separate pan with 300ml of water and bring it to boil and simmer for 20-25 minutes, strain the water though a fine sieve and keep aside. Slice the garlic and shallots and julienne the ginger.
2. Heat the oil in a separate pan. Add the fenugreek seeds, cook on a medium heat and allow to turn dark brown to release their flavour. Now add the mustard seeds and turn the heat up until the seeds pop. Add the garlic and cook until golden brown. Add the ginger, curry leaves and shallots and cook further for another 7-10 minutes until the shallots are light brown.
3. Lower the heat and add the Kashmiri chilli powder, turmeric powder, salt and tomato paste. Add the sieved tamarind and coccum water and another 400ml of water. Bring to boil, then simmer for 20-25 minutes until the sauce reaches the desired consistency. Add the cubed monkfish fillets and simmer for another 5-6 minutes.
4. Check the seasoning and serve hot.

COCONUT CHILLI PRAWNS

What you'll need

Portion – 7
King prawn – 28 pieces (cleaned and deveined)
Oil – 100ml
Lemon grass – 13gms (1 stick)
Galangal – 40gms
Curry leaves – 4gms
Kaffir lime leaves – 4gms (4piece)
Onions – 750gms
Lee Kum Kee chilli garlic sauce – 100gms
Kashmiri chilli powder – 10gms
Turmeric powder – 5gms
Salt – 10gms
Tomato puree – 100gms
Coconut milk powder – 200gms

How it's done

1. Mix the coconut milk powder with 400ml of water and keep aside.
2. Chop the onions and slice the lemon grass and galangal.
3. Heat the oil in a pan and add the lemon grass, galangal, kaffir lime leaves and curry leaves.
4. Add the onions and sauté for approximately 20 minutes, so that the onions become soft and cooked but not browned. Lower the flame and add the Kashmiri chilli powder, turmeric powder, salt, chilli garlic sauce and tomato puree and stir for a couple of minutes.
5. Now add the coconut milk and simmer the sauce for another 15-20 minutes.
6. Once the sauce is ready poach the king prawns in the sauce for another 3-4 minutes.
7. Check the seasoning and serve hot.

TANDOORI KING PRAWNS AND SEAFOOD RISOTTO

What you'll need

Portion – 6
King prawns – 24pcs (6-8 size) cleaned and de-veined and slit from the centre to the bottom.
Mustard paste
Oil – 25ml
Green chilli chopped – 5gms
Ginger chopped – 8gms
Whole grain mustard – 60gms

English mustard – 40gms
Turmeric powder – 2gms
Salt – 2gms

Ginger chopped – 2gms
Green chilli chopped – 2gms
Hung yoghurt – 40gms
Salt – 2gms
Chopped coriander leaves – 3gms

How it's done

1. Heat the oil in a pan. Add chopped ginger and chopped green chilli. Stir for a minute.
2. Add whole grain mustard and mustard paste, turmeric and salt and cook on a low heat for 8-10 minutes. Allow to cool.
3. In a separate bowl mix the cooked mustard paste with the second set of ingredients, which are those listed from chopped ginger to chopped coriander leaves. Add the prawns to marinade.

Seafood Risotto

What you'll need

For the risotto:
Basmati rice – 150gms
Vegetable oil – 25ml
Ginger chopped – 4gms
Green chilli chopped – 2gms
Curry leaves chopped – 2gms
Shallots sliced – 30gms
Mustard seeds – 2gms
Urad dal split – 4gms
Fish cubes – 10gms
Salt – 2gms
Water – 250ml

Red onions chopped – 25gms
Coriander leaves chopped – 5gms
Butter unsalted – 20gms
Cream single – 100ml
Cooked shrimps – 100gms
Water – 100ml

How it's done

1. Wash the rice a couple of times to remove any dust and dirt. Soak the rice in water for at least an hour. Heat oil in separate pan and add the urad dal. Allow it to turn golden brown then add the mustard seeds and allow them to crackle. Add the chopped ginger, green chilli, curry leaves and shallots and sauté for couple of minutes. Now add the 250ml of water along with the salt and fish cubes. Bring to the boil.
2. Drain the rice in a colander and place it in boiling water. Stir one or two times without breaking the grains. Once the water starts evaporating and you can see the rice clearly, cover the pan with a lid and keep it on a very low heat for 7-8 minutes. Check the rice. Once just cooked remove it from the heat but but keep the lid on.
3. In a separate pan add the water, single cream and butter and bring to the boil. Add the cooked rice followed by the shrimps, red onions and coriander leaves. Once well mixed take off the heat. Divide into 6 portions.
4. Preheat the oven to 180C and cook the prawns for 4-6 minutes.

To serve

1. To serve, plate the risotto rice in the middle of the plate with a steel ring with approximately (125gms) per portion. Add 4 cooked prawns per portion as in photograph with salad leaves for garnish.

PRAWN MOILEE

What you'll need

Portion – 4
Prawns (16-20 size) – 20 pcs
Oil – 30ml
Garlic – 30gms
Ginger – 10gms
Green chilli – 6gms
Curry leaves – 2gms
Onion – 100gms
Turmeric powder – 6gms
Salt – 10gms
Coconut milk powder – 250gms

How it's done

1. Peel and de-vein the prawns, wash thoroughly and keep to one side.
2. Slice the onions and garlic, julienne the ginger and slit the green chillies.
3. Blend the coconut milk powder with 800ml of hot water and keep to one side.
4. Heat the oil in a pan then add in the garlic and cook until it turns a light brown. Mix in the ginger, green chillies, onions and curry leaves and sauté for a couple of minutes.
5. Lower the heat and add the turmeric powder. Keep on a low flame and make sure you do not burn the turmeric. Add the coconut milk and salt and bring to the boil. Allow to simmer for 10-12 minutes.
6. Once you have checked the seasoning, mix in the prawns and cook it in the sauce for approximately four to five minutes. Serve hot.

MALABAR FISH CURRY

What you'll need

Portions – 4
Halibut steaks – 600gms (skinned and boned)
Onion – 100gms
Ginger – 20gms
Green chilli – 12gms
Kashmiri chilli powder – 20gms
Turmeric powder – 5gms
Oil – 50ml
Fenugreek seeds – 2gms
Curry leaves – 2gms
Tomato – 200gms
Coconut paste – 30gms (base recipe)

Salt – 20gms
Tamarind – 30gms
Coconut milk powder – 100gms
kodumpuli/coccum – 5gms
Fennel powder – 1gm
Water – 200ml

TEMPERING
Coconut oil – 50ml
Shallots – 80gms
Kashmiri chilli powder – 5gms
Curry leaves – 2gms

How it's done

1. Slice the onions and shallots, julienne the ginger, slit the green chilli and chop the tomatoes. Cut the fish into small cubes that are each about 50gms.
2. Soak the tamarind in 300ml of warm water for at least half an hour so that the pulp develops a strong flavour and is easy to extract.
3. Soak the coccum in warm water in a separate bowl.
4. Mix the coconut milk powder with 200ml of water and blend it well.
5. Heat the oil and add the fenugreek seeds. Once they turn golden brown place the onion, ginger and green chilli into the pan and cook for approximately 10 minutes on a medium heat. Add the curry leaves, Kashmiri chilli powder and turmeric powder. Stir fry on a low heat without burning the powdered masala. Now add the tomatoes and salt and cook until the tomatoes mash. Add 200ml of water and allow the onions and tomatoes to form a thick sauce. Add the tamarind pulp and cocccum pieces and allow to simmer.
6. Check the seasoning. Add the fish cubes and cook for 2- 3 minutes. Once the fish is half done add the coconut paste, coconut milk and fennel powder. Bring to the boil then take off the heat.
7. For tempering: heat the oil in a separate pan and add the sliced shallots. Fry until golden brown. Add the Kashmiri chilli powder and curry leaves and pour the tempering over the fish curry. Serve hot.

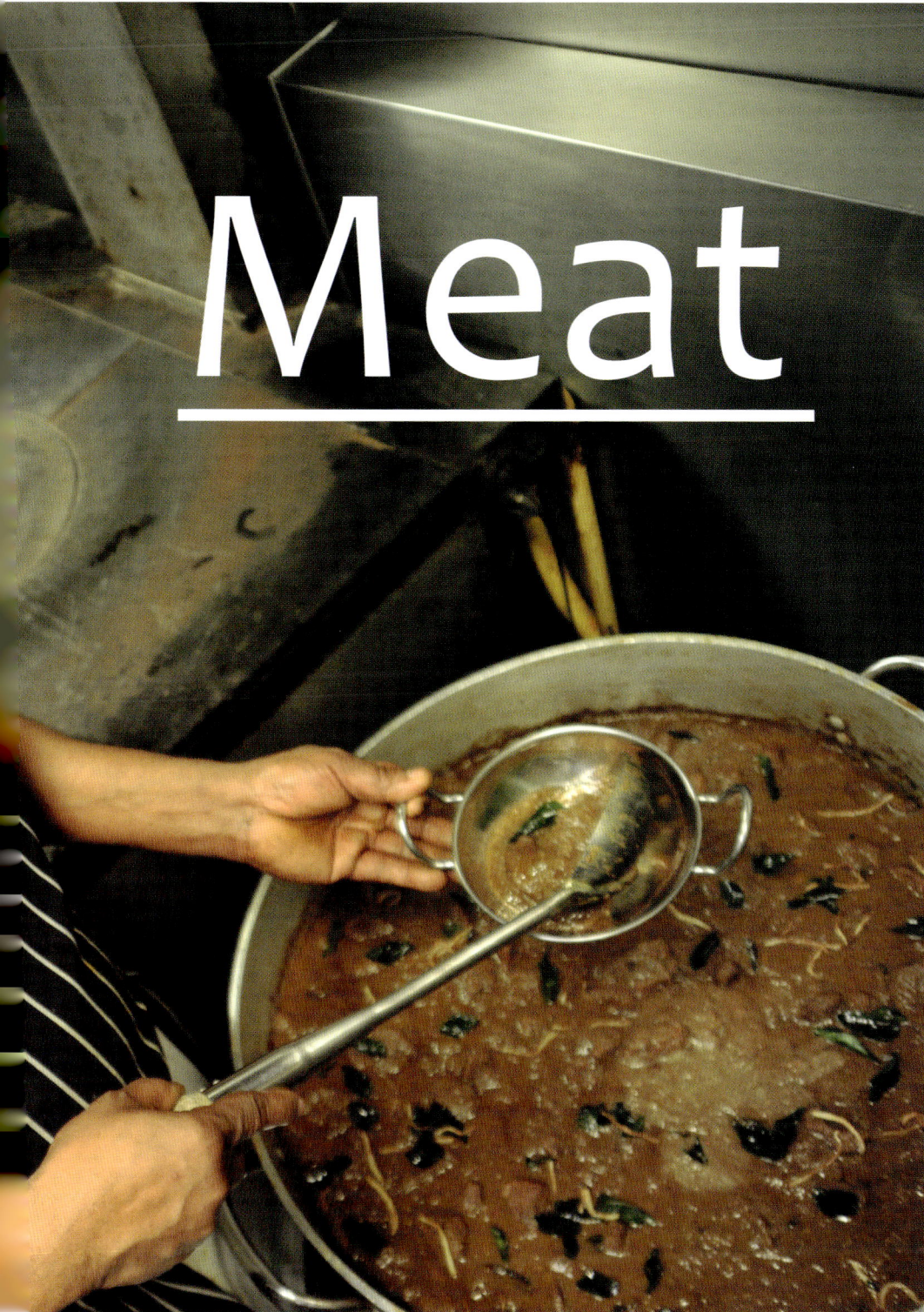

Meat

MALABAR LAMB BIRYANI

What you'll need

Portion – 6
Lamb leg, boneless – 1250gms
Onions – 1kg
Garlic – 40gms
Ginger – 50gms
Green Chilli – 60gms
Mint leaves – 25gms
Coriander leaves – 30gms
Turmeric powder – 10gms
Yoghurt – 600gms
Salt – 20gms
Tomato – 100gms
Butter ghee – 100gms
Fennel seeds – 5gms
Desiccated coconut paste – 50gms (base recipe)
Lamb stock – 800ml

How it's done

1. Trim the lamb leg, and cut into cubes weighing approximately 50gms each. There should be around 25 pieces.
2. Slice the onions and chop the ginger, green chilli and garlic.
3. Chop the mint and coriander leaves.
4. In a thick-bottomed pan mix all of the remaining ingredients, except lamb stock. Keep it on the heat, stirring constantly. When the onion starts softening, after approximately 20 minutes, add the lamb stock. Bring it to the boil and cover it with a lid. Keep it on a low flame, stirring regularly for at least an hour until the lamb is tender. Remove from the heat.

Basmati Rice

What you'll need

Basmati Rice – 1200gms
Green Cardamom – 2gms
Bay leaf – 2 pieces
Cloves- –1gm
Mace – 1 piece
Cinnamon – 2gms
Butter ghee – 150gms
Water – 1600ml
Salt – 30gms

How it's done

1. Wash the rice three times to remove the dirt and dust, and soak it for an hour.
2. Strain the soaked rice in a sieve.
3. Heat the butter ghee in a thick-bottomed pan. Add whole spices and allow to crackle so that they release their flavour. Now add 1600ml of water and salt and bring to boil. Add the rice and allow it to cook. When the water evaporates and the rice rises to the top cover the pan with a lid and keep it on a low flame for 10 minutes. Take off the flame and keep aside with the lid on.

Garam Masala Powder

What you'll need

Mace – 3gms
Green cardamom – 15gms
Fennel seeds – 20gms
Cloves – 3gms
Cinnamon – 3gms

How it's done

1. Combine the spices and grind until they are a fine powder. Set aside. You will need them for the final finish.

For the final finish

What you'll need

Chopped pineapple – 50gms
Chopped mint – 20gms
Chopped coriander – 20gms
Fried onion – 40gms
Rose water – 5ml
Saffron water – 5ml
Garam Masala Powder – use 10gms of the powder from the recipe on the facing page and reserve the remainder for use later.

How it's done

1. Bring the lamb mixture to heat, once it starts bubbling take off the heat.
2. Add the chopped pineapple, half of the mint, coriander, fried onion and garam masala powder to the cooked lamb mixture. Add half of the cooked rice, top it up with mint, coriander, fried onion and garam masala powder. Add the rest of the rice and sprinkle rose water and saffron water into the mix.
3. Cover it with lid and keep on a low heat for 10 minutes. Then remove from the heat and keep it covered with a lid for at least half an hour.
4. You can serve the biryani in a copper bowl with a flat bread on top (as in the photograph on the previous page.

KASHMIRI ROGANJOSH

What you'll need

Portion – 6
Lamb leg, boneless – 1450gms
Clean and trim the lamb and cut it into cubes. There should be approximately 24 pieces of 60gms each
Fried garlic – 70gms (base recipe)
Fried onion – 200gms (base recipe)
Vegetable oil – 50ml
Cinnamon – 4gms
Black cardamom – 2gms
Cloves – 1gm
Bay leaf – 3 pieces
Mace – 2 pieces
Star anise – 2 pieces
Ginger garlic paste – 30gms (base recipe)
Kashmiri chilli powder – 5gms

Turmeric powder – 3gms
Coriander powder – 12gms
Kitchen King – 8gms
Salt – 15gms
Kashmiri red chilli paste – 35gms (base recipe)
Lamb stock – 1500ml
Tomato paste – 80gms
Yoghurt – 80gms (blend it well with a whisk)
Water 300 ml
Green cardamom powder – 1gm
Saffron powder – 1gm
Fennel powder – 1gm

How it's done

1. In a bowl mix the fried garlic and fried onion and add some lukewarm water, wash and drain it in a sieve to remove the excess oil. Add 300ml of lukewarm water and set it aside for 10-15 minutes then blend it to fine paste.
2. Heat oil in thick-bottomed pan. Add first selection of spices, from cinnamon to star anise in the list above, and allow them to release their flavour into the oil.
3. Then add the ginger garlic paste. Keep stirring until it turns golden brown. Now place the lamb cubes into the mix and keep on braising it on a high heat for 5-10 minutes without burning.
4. Once the lamb is braised, add Kashmiri chilli powder, turmeric powder, coriander powder, kitchen king, red chilli paste and salt. Keep on stirring on a low heat. Add tomato paste, yoghurt, onion and garlic paste.
5. Now add the lamb stock and bring it boil. Add 300ml of water as well. Cover it with a lid and keep it simmering for approximately an hour.
6. Once the lamb is tender, take off the heat. With a ladle take out all the cooked lamb from the sauce and cover with cling film and keep aside. Remove the whole spices that have stuck to the cooked lamb. Meanwhile pass the sauce through the sieve and throw away the whole spices.
7. Blend the sauce with the green cardamom, saffron and fennel powder and add the lamb cubes back to sauce, bring to boil. Check the seasoning and serve hot.

RAANAKBARI

What you'll need

Portion – 6
Lamb Shank 450gms each – 6pcs
Salt – 10gms
Onions – 500gms
Tomato – 200gms
Oil –100ml
Cinnamon – 6gms
Bay leaf – 5 pieces
Green cardamom – 2gms

Cloves – 1gm
Ginger garlic paste – 50gms
Kashmiri chilli powder – 20gms
Turmeric powder – 10gms
Salt – 8gms
Lamb stock – 2litre
Water – 2litre
Melted butter – 12ml
Gram flour – 5gms

How it's done

1. Clean and trim the lamb shank to remove skin and fat. Season with salt and leave for an hour. Wash the lamb shank in running water and drain in a colander.
2. Grind onions and tomatoes to a fine paste
3. Heat the oil in a pan. Add the cinnamon, bay leaf, green cardamom and cloves and allow them to release their flavour to oil.
4. Now add the lamb shank and saute for a couple of minutes.
5. Add the ginger garlic paste and saute for a couple of minutes. Add the Kashmiri chilli powder, turmeric powder, salt and onion and tomato paste and stir for 7-8 minutes.
6. Now add the lamb stock and one litre of water and simmer the lamb shank with a lid on for an hour.
7. Add one more litre of water and simmer for another hour. The lamb shank should be tender and holding onto the bone.
8. Take the pan off the heat and separate the lamb shank from the sauce.
9. Cover with cling film and allow to cool. Strain the sauce.
10. Heat the butter in a pan, add the gram flour and cook on a low heat like a roux for a minute without burning. Now add the strained sauce and bring to the boil. Check the seasoning and consistency of the sauce.

Butternut Squash Mash

What you'll need

Butternut Squash– 1 (450-500gms)
Peeled, seeds removed and cubed net weight will be 350-400gms
Oil-10gms
Salt-6gms

How it's done

1. Preheat the oven to 180C. Mix the butternut squash cubes with salt and oil and place it in a tray and roast for 15-20 minutes until soft enough to mash.
2. Take off the oven and place the butternut squash in a pan. With the back of a ladle, mash the roasted butternut squash while it is on a low heat. Remove the excess moisture of the mash for another 10 minutes and keep aside.
3. Meanwhile, prepare the tempering.

Tempering

What you'll need

Vegetable oil – 20ml
Mustard seeds – 2gms
Curry leaves chopped – 2gms
Green chilli chopped – 2gms
Ginger chopped – 6gms
Urad dal split – 4gms
Grated potatoes – 400gms (base recipe)
Turmeric powder – 1gm
Salt – 2gms

How it's done

1. Heat the oil in pan and add the urad dal and allow it to brown.
2. Then add the mustard seeds and allow to crackle.
3. Then add the chopped ginger, green chilli and curry leaves. Lower the heat and add the turmeric powder and salt.
4. Now add the grated potatoes and the butternut squash. Mix well, check the seasoning and keep aside. Divide it into 6 portions (90gms per portion).

To Serve

1. To serve preheat the oven to 250C roast the lamb shank for 4-5 minutes, then lower the temperature to 180C and cook for another4-5 minutes to make it crisp on the outside and still juicy inside. Baste it with clarified butter and chat masala.
2. Reheat the sauce in a separate pan.
3. Plate as in photograph with the mint sorbet (base recipe), sauce and butternut squash quenelle alongside the lamb.

CHEFSIDDARTHA
LAALMAAS

What you'll need

Portion – 6

Lamb leg, boneless – 1440gms
Oil – 100ml
Onions – 400gms
Bay leaf – 2gms
Black cardamom – 4gms
Ginger garlic paste – 50gms

Red chilli paste – 60gms (base recipe)
Salt – 15gms
Kashmiri chilli powder – 15gms
Coriander powder – 20gms
Turmeric powder – 5gms
Yoghurt – 150gms
Tomato puree – 70gms
Lamb stock – 1500ml

How it's done

1. Clean and trim the lamb and cut it into cubes. There should be approximately 24 pieces of 60gms each
2. Slice the onions and heat the oil in a thick-bottomed pan. Add the bay leaf and black cardamom. Allow the spices to release their flavour to the oil. Now add the sliced onions and stir constantly until light brown, which should take ten minutes. Now add the lamb cubes and keep on stirring for another ten minutes until the onion goes very soft. Add 100 ml of stock and keep stirring. After five minutes add the ginger garlic paste and keep on stirring.
3. Add 100 ml of lamb stock, whisk the yoghurt, keep aside. Now lower the heat and add the red chilli paste, Kashmiri chilli powder, coriander powder, turmeric powder, salt and keep on stirring the lamb, now add the tomato puree and yoghurt, rest of the lamb stock bring back to boil then simmer it on a medium heat with lid on for an hour.
4. Check the lamb to see it is tender and cooked. Keep aside from the heat.

Tempering

Oil – 25ml
Cloves – 1gm
Garlic chopped – 15gms
Whole red dry Kashmiri chilli – 5gms (2 pieces)

1. Heat the oil in a separate pan. Add the cloves and chopped garlic. Allow the garlic to turn brown. Now add the red chilli. Stir for a minute then pour over the cooked lamb curry.

LAMBULARTHIYATHU
(Lamb Coconut Fry)

What you'll need

Portion – 4
Welsh Lamb leg boneless – 1.5kg
Onions sliced – 550gms
Tomato chopped – 150gms
Curry leaves – 4gms
Kashmiri chilli powder – 5gms
Turmeric powder – 2gms
Coriander powder – 15gms
Salt – 15gms
Ginger garlic paste – 30gms
Lamb stock – 1000ml
Fennel seeds – 4gms
Coconut oil – 25ml
Coconut chips – 50ml (available in Asian markets or else crack a coconut and cut the flesh into small cubes)

How it's done

1. Trim and clean the lamb leg and cut into small cubes. There should be approximately 36 pieces of lamb, each weighing just over 40gms each.
2. In a thick-bottomed pan place the lamb leg cubes with sliced onions, tomatoes, ginger garlic paste, chilli powder, turmeric powder, coriander powder, salt, fennel seeds, curry leaves, coconut chips, coconut oil and salt. Mix together and keep stirring on a high heat for 15-20 minutes.
3. Now add the lamb stock and bring it to the boil. Cover it with a lid and keep simmering for at least an hour until the lamb is tender and firm. Keep aside from the heat.

For the stir fry

What you'll need

Garlic – 30gms
Ginger – 16gms
Green Chilli – 10gms
Madras onions – 200gms
Coconut oil – 50ml (can be substituted
with any vegetable oil, though the
authentic way features coconut oil)

Curry leaves – 4gms
Garam masala powder – Keralan style
–2gms (base recipe)
Black pepper powder – 4gms

How it's done

1. Slice the madras onions, garlic, julienne the ginger and slit the green chilli.
2. Heat the coconut oil in a separate pan. Add the garlic and stir until light brown. Place the ginger julienne, slit green chilli and add the curry leaves and Madras onions into the pan and stir fry for 10-15 minutes until the mixture starts to turn brown. Now add the cooked lamb mixture and keep on stirring on a low heat for another 15 minutes until the masala coats the lamb. Finish it with a sprinkling of garam masala powder and black pepper powder.
3. Check the seasoning and serve hot.

KERALAN HOMESTYLE LAMB CURRY

What you'll need

Portion – 6
Shoulder of lamb – 1.3kg (skin removed, cleaned and trimmed)
Onions, sliced – 500gms
Tomato chopped – 50gms
Kashmiri chilli powder – 6gms
Turmeric powder – 4gms
Coriander powder- 20gms
Salt – 12gms
Ginger garlic paste – 20gms
Fennel seeds – 2gms
Lamb stock – 1000 - 1200ml
Potatoes – 350gms
Coconut oil – 25ml
Coconut milk powder – 50gms
Curry leaves – 4gms

How it's done

1. Cut the lamb shoulder into small cubes. You should have approximately 26 pieces of 50gms each.
2. Peel the potato and cut it into cubes.
3. Blend the coconut milk powder with 100 ml of lukewarm water.
4. In a pan mix the lamb cubes with the onion, tomatoes, curry leaves, Kashmiri chilli powder, turmeric powder, coriander powder, fennel seeds, salt and ginger garlic paste and 25ml of coconut oil.
5. Sear the lamb and keep stirring continuously until the masala starts coating the lamb. After 10-15 minutes add the lamb stock and cook the lamb on a low heat with a lid on for an approximately 40-50 minutes.
6. When the lamb is just done, add the potato and the coconut milk and bring it to boil, then simmer for another 10 minutes until the potato is just cooked.

Tempering

What you'll need

Coconut oil – 25ml
Ginger – 10gms
Garlic – 5gms
Green chilli – 4gms
Garam masala powder Keralan style (base recipe) – 4gms
Shallots – 50gms
Curry leaves – 3gms
Kashmiri chilli powder – 4gms

How it's done

1. For tempering slice the shallots and garlic, slit the green chilli and julienne the ginger.
2. In separate pan heat the oil then add the sliced garlic and keep stir-frying until it turns light golden brown. Then add the ginger julienne, slit green chilli, curry leaves and shallots. Stir fry until it turns light brown. Add Kashmiri chilli powder to the cooked lamb and sprinkle with garam masala powder.
3. Check seasoning and serve hot.

LOIN⦿OFLAMB

What you'll need

Portion – 5
Loin of lamb – 800-850gms
Lamb mince – 200gms (minced trimmings)
Onions sliced – 200gms
Oil – 25ml
Fennel seeds – 1gm
Salt – 2gms
Crushed black pepper powder – 2gms
Turmeric powder – 1gm
Kashmiri chilli powder – 1gm
Coriander powder – 3gms
Ginger garlic paste – 8gms
Fennel powder – 2gms
Tomato puree – 30gms
Water – 200ml

How it's done

1. To begin, prepare the lamb loin, clean all the fat and sinew from the loins. Set aside the trimmings for the mince (200gms).
2. Cling film the loin (400-425gm) and keep it in the refrigerator.
3. Meanwhile start making the mince mixture.
4. Heat the oil in a thick-bottomed pan. Add the sliced onions and cook for 15 minutes until light golden brown.
5. Now add the lamb mince and fennel seeds and braise for a further 3- 4 minutes. Add the ginger garlic paste and cook until the raw smells disappear and it starts catching the bottom of the pan.
6. Now lower the heat and add the turmeric powder, coriander powder, Kashmiri chilli powder and salt and stir for a minute without burning the powdered spices. Add the tomato puree and cook further.
7. Add the water, 200ml initially, and bring it to the boil. Cover it with a lid and simmer for 10-12 minutes.
8. Once the lamb mince is cooked, sprinkle with fennel powder. Allow the mixture to cool and divide into five portions. The yield is 200gms.

Sauce

Lamb stock – 400ml
Butter – 30ml
Gram flour – 15gms
Chatpata sauce – 150gms (base recipe)
Water – 200ml

1. In a pan make a roux with the butter and gram flour. Add the lamb stock and bring to the boil. Add the chatpata sauce and simmer for an hour. Strain the sauce and keep aside. The yield of the sauce is enough for five portions.

Chickpeas and Kale Masala

Boiled chickpeas – 60gms
Kale – 60gms
Chatpata sauce– 100gms (base recipe)

1. Blanch the kale and drain in a colander. Heat the sauce in a pan along with the chickpeas. Add the blanched kale and mix it well. Take off the heat and keep aside.

Sweetbreads

Sweetbreads – 160gms
Crushed coriander seeds – 1gm
Crushed fennel seeds – 1gm
Turmeric powder – 1gm
Salt – 1gm
Plain flour – 10gms

1. Blanch the sweetbreads for two minutes. Cool and remove the skin and sinew. Mix with the remaining ingredients.
2. Divide it into 5 portions.

To serve

Salt
Butter

1. Cook the lamb loin in a pan and season well on both sides. Add the butter and cook gently for 3-4 minutes on each side and rest for 10 minutes.
2. In another pan, fry the sweetbreads in more butter for 2-3 minutes and keep aside.
3. Reheat the sauce, lamb mince, masala chickpeas and kale and divide into 5 portions.
4. To assemble, make a quenelle of lamb mince then add the chickpeas and kale masala, sweetbreads and loin as shown in the picture. Add the sauce. Serve hot.

NAWABI MURG

How it's done

Portion – 5

1. Take 5 pieces of chicken supreme (250-280gm each) and remove the skin and inner supreme but keep the shoulder bone on. Make a slit in the chicken supreme so that the marinade can penetrate the meat more easily.
2. To make the first marinade take: Salt – 4gms; Lemon juice – 15ml; Vegetable oil – 20ml; Ginger garlic paste – 30gms. Marinate the chicken supreme with the above for an hour.
3. In separate bowl mix the following: Cardamom powder – 2gms; Mace powder – 1gm; Ginger chopped – 10gms; Green chilli chopped – 6gms; Coriander leaves chopped – 5gms; Hung yoghurt – 40gms; Philadelphia Cheese – 110gms (medium fat cheese); single cream – 25ml.
4. Add that mixture to the chicken supreme and marinate for six hours or overnight.

Bhuno Thigh

What you'll need

First marinade
Chicken thigh – 800gms (15 pieces of thigh, 3 pieces of thigh per portion)
Ginger garlic paste – 35gms
Lemon juice – 25ml
Mustard oil – 25ml
Salt – 5gms

How it's done

1. Marinade the thighs with the above and keep it refrigerated for 1-2 hours.
2. In separate bowl mix the following: Kashmiri chilli powder – 15gms; hung yoghurt – 120gms; chat masala – 2gms; amchur powder – 2gms; chana masala powder – 2gms; kasoori methi leaves – 2gms.
3. Add this mixture to the chicken supreme, keep for 6 hours.
4. To cook, preheat the oven to 240C, place the chicken thighs in a roasting tray and roast the for 5 minutes to give colour, then lower the oven temperature to 180C and cook for 8-10 minutes, rest the chicken thigh after cooking. Also, cook the chicken supreme.
5. Now you'll need Chatpata sauce – 300gms (base recipe).
6. Take the cooked chicken thighs and cut into thick julienne. In a pan add the chatpata sauce. Loosen it with a little water. Add the chicken julienne and stir fry for a minute.
7. Reheat makhani sauce – 400gms (base recipe).

To serve

1. To serve place the stir fry thigh on the left hand corner of the plate followed by the chicken supreme and on the right hand corner. Add the makhani sauce followed by the mint sorbet (base recipe).

HOMESTYLE CHICKEN CURRY

What you'll need

Portion – 6
Dry roast spices:
Desiccated coconut, fine – 150gms
Fennel seeds – 2gms
Curry leaves – 2gms
Coriander powder– 8gms
Turmeric powder – 2gms
Kashmiri chilli powder – 5gms

Chicken thigh, boneless – 1.3kg
Cleaned and trimmed with each thigh cut
into 2 pieces.

Oil – 50ml
Onions – 220gms
Cinnamon – 1gm
Green cardamom – 1gm
Cloves – 1gm

Bayleaf – 3pcs
Green chilli – 5gms
Curry leaves – 2gms
Ginger garlic paste – 30gms
Chicken stock – 1litre
Salt – 12gms
Coconut milk powder – 70gms

For tempering:
Coconut oil – 25ml
Ginger julienne – 10gms
Mustard seeds – 2gms
Curry leaves – 2gms
Madras onions, sliced – 40gms
Kashmiri chilli powder – 2gms
Garam masala powder – Keralan style
–2gms (base recipe)

How it's done

1. Dry roast the first set of ingredients on a low heat for 7-8 minutes and grind into a fine paste with 300ml of water.
2. Slice the onions, slit the green chilli and blend the coconut milk powder with 150ml of water.
3. Heat the oil in a pan. Add the cinnamon, cardamom, cloves and bay leaf and allow them to release their flavours into the oil. Add the green chilli and curry leaves and saute for a minute. Now add the sliced onions and saute for another 12-15 minutes until the onions are light brown. Now add the ginger garlic paste. Stir it for a minute then add the stock, starting with 600ml and bringing to a boil. Add the ground coconut paste and salt and cook for another 15 minutes. Once the sauce thickens add the rest of the stock. Now add the chicken thigh and coconut milk and cook for another 10-12minutes. Once the chicken is just done prepare for the tempering.
4. Heat the oil in a separate pan. Allow the mustard seeds to pop up and then add the sliced shallots and ginger and stir fry until golden brown. Add the curry leaves. Lower the heat and add the Kashmiri chilli powder and garam masala powder. Pour the tempering into the cooked chicken curry.
5. Check seasoning and serve hot.

TANDOORICHICKEN

Portion – 4
Take a whole chicken, weighing about 1.2kg, with the head, feet, wings and giblets removed. The breast and legs should be scored to allow the marinade to seep in.

First marinade

Ginger garlic paste – 30gms
Salt – 5gms
Kashmiri chilli powder –7gms
Lemon juice – 15ml
Mustard oil – 15ml

Apply this marinade on the chicken and leave for an hour.

Second marinade

Ginger garlic paste – 15gms
Hung yoghurt – 250gms
Kasoori methi leaves – 2gms
Salt – 5gms
Kashmiri chilli powder – 20gms
Chana masala powder – 2gms
Amchur powder – 1gm
Chat masala – 2gms
Mustard oil – 10ml

Mix the above marinade in a bowl. Run through your fingers until smooth and rub it into the chicken, leaving for three hours or overnight in the fridge.

Preheat the oven to 250C. Place the chicken on a wire mesh then place it on top of a roasting tray, with the breast side facing up. Roast the chicken for 5 minutes to get a nice colour. Now lower the temperature to 180 C and roast for another 12-15 minute but baste with melted butter every 5 minutes to keep the moisture on and avoid it drying out. Leave the chicken to rest for 2-3 minutes.
Now carve the chicken and serve with Mixed salad (base recipe), Mint sauce (base recipe), Pickled red onion (base recipe), Pickled cucumber (base recipe).

Anand George

MURGTIKKALABABDAR

What you'll need

Portion – 4
Murg tikka
Chicken supreme – 800gms (3pcs)

Trim the chicken supreme and cut each one into four pieces. Each piece should be approximately 65gms.

First marinade

Kashmiri chilli powder – 10gms
Kasoori methi leaves– 2gms
Ginger garlic paste – 20gms
Lemon juice – 10ml
Mustard oil – 15ml
Salt – 3gms

In a separate bowl mix the chicken pieces with the above ingredients and leave for at least 2 hours.

Second marinade

Hung yoghurt – 150gms
Kashmiri chilli powder – 6gms
Kasoori methi leaves – 2gms
Chana masala powder – 1gm
Ginger garlic paste – 15gms

Mustard oil – 10ml
Salt – 3gms
Amchur powder – 1gm
Chat masala – 1gm

In a separate bowl combine the above and add it to the first marinated chicken, keep the chicken marinated for at least 2 hours

Chatpata sauce – 400gms
Makhani sauce – 600gms
Green chilli sliced – 6gms
Ginger julienne – 10gms

Coriander leaves chopped – 5gms
Kasoori methi leaves – 2gms
Unsalted butter – 10gms
Single cream – 50gms

How it's done

Pre heat the oven to 250C and roast for the chicken for 5 minutes. Baste it with melted butter. Lower the temperature to 180C and cook for another 5 minutes until cooked through. Sprinkle with chat masala and melted butter.

In a thick-bottomed pan, heat the chatpata and makhani sauce together, then add the green chilli, ginger, butter, kasoori methi leaves, single cream and coriander leaves. Add the cooked chicken tikka, check the seasoning and serve hot.

MURGH KOFTA
KHORMA

What you'll need

Portion – 5
Oil
Kofta (20 pieces)
Chicken mince – 550gms
Ginger, chopped – 10gms
Green chilli, chopped – 4gms
Coriander leaves, chopped – 5gms
Salt – 3gms
Single cream – 25ml

Stuffing:
Prunes – 100gms (seedless and chopped)
Mint, chopped – 2gms

Water – 2.5 litre
Bay leaf – 2gms
Green cardamom – 2gms
Cloves – 2gms
Cinnamon stick – 4gms
Salt – 10gms
Coriander stem – 25gms

How it's done

1. Mix the chicken mince with the ginger, green chilli, coriander leaves, salt and single cream and divide into 20 balls of 30gms each. Keep aside.
2. Mix the prunes and mint together and divide into 20 portion of 5gms each.
3. Apply some oil to your hands and place the chicken mince into your palm. Flatten it a bit then put the prune and mint filling in the middle. Shape it like a ball. Make 19 more and keep them separately in a tray so that they don't stick together or lose shape.
4. Meanwhile make the cooking water to blanch the stuffed chicken balls. Place all of the remaining ingredients (from water to coriander stem) in a pan and bring to the boil. Keep simmering for 10-15 minutes to flavour the liquor. Now add the chicken mince balls and blanch them for 2 minutes, strain and add to the sauce.

Khorma Sauce

What you'll need

Onions sliced – 850gms
Cashew nuts – 150gms (broken)
Water – 800ml
Oil – 25ml
Ginger garlic paste – 30gms
Green chilli chopped – 10gms

Chicken stock – 700ml
Salt – 10gms
Single cream – 200ml
Green cardamom powder – 2gms
Rose water – 5ml

How it's done

1. In a separate pan boil the sliced onions, cashew nut and water for 25-30 minutes and take off the fire and blend to a fine paste.
2. Heat the oil in a separate pan, add the ginger garlic paste and sauté for couple of minutes until light brown. Add the chopped green chilli, cooked blended paste and chicken stock. Bring to the boil and simmer for another 25-30 minutes. Take off the heat and strain the sauce with a fine sieve until smooth consistency. Bring back to boil, finish with single cream, green cardamom powder and rose water.
3. Add the blanched chicken mince kofta into the sauce and serve four kofta per portion. Garnish with fried onions and microcress.
4. Serve hot.

BEEFSTEW

What you'll need

Portion – 6
Rump of beef – 1260gms
Shin bones – 6 pieces
Water – 1800ml
Black peppercorns – 2gms
Cinnamon – 4gms
Green Cardamom – 2gms
Cloves – 1gm
Salt – 12gms
Ginger – 40gms
Green chilli – 25gms
Curry leaves – 3gms
Onions – 300gms
Oil – 25ml
Coconut milk powder – 200gms

How it's done

1. Clean and trim the rump and cut into cubes until you have approximately 30 pieces of 40gms each.
2. In a thick-bottomed pan, place the beef cubes along with the shin bones and cover with cold water and bring it to the boil for ten minutes to remove any impurities. Take off the heat and discard the water. Wash the beef beneath running water.
3. In a clean pan, place the beef cubes and shin bones along with 1500ml of water and add black peppercorns, cinnamon, green cardamom, cloves and salt.
4. Bring it to the boil and cover it with a lid. Simmer for approximately an hour.
5. Slice the onions, slit the green chilli and julienne ginger.
6. In a separate pan heat the oil and add the onions, ginger, green chilli and curry leaves. Saute for few minutes and then add to the simmering beef pot. Add 300ml of water and keep cooking on a high flame for another 10 minutes so that the onion mixture cooks well.
7. Blend the coconut milk powder with 300 ml of water and keep aside.
8. Add the coconut milk into beef pot and simmering for another 10-15 minutes. Remove from the heat and discard the shin bones.

Tempering

Madras onions – 50gms (or use banana shallots)
Pure butter ghee – 50gms
Golden raisins – 50gms
Cashew nuts – 30gms
Curry leaves – 2gms
Black pepper powder – 4gms

1. Slice the Madras onions.
2. In a separate pan heat the butter ghee and add the madras onions and allow to turn golden brown. Add the raisins and cashew nuts and stir fry for a minute.
3. Now add the curry leaves and sprinkle the black peppercorn powder.
4. Add it to the cooked beef stew. Check the consistency of the sauce, seasoning and serve hot.

BEEFKURUMELAGU

Portion – 4
Rump of beef – 1.35kg
Onions – 1.2kg
Cinnamon – 2gms
Green cardamom – 2gms
Cloves – 2gms
Bay leaf – 1gm
Vegetable oil – 60ml
Ginger – 20gms
Green chilli – 10gms
Curry leaves – 2gms
Salt – 12gms

Tomato – 50gms
Ginger garlic paste – 30gms
Fennel seeds – 2gms
Turmeric powder – 4gms
Coriander powder – 20gms
Beef stock – 500ml
Black peppercorns – 8gms
Fried onion – 90gms (base recipe)
Garam masala powder – Keralan style – 2gms (base recipe)
Water – 200ml

How it's done

1. Clean and trim the rump and cut into cubes, yielding approximately 30 pieces of 45gms each.
2. Slice the onions and tomatoes. Slit the green chilli and julienne the ginger.
3. In a thick-bottomed pan heat the oil along with the cinnamon, cardamom, cloves and bayleaf on a medium heat. Add the ginger julienne, slit green chilli and curry leaves. Stir for a minute and add the sliced onions and salt. Cook for half an hour, stirring regularly. The onions will reduce. Gradually mash the onions and add the ginger garlic paste and stir for a minute. Add the coriander powder and turmeric powder and saute. Add the sliced tomatoes and the cubed beef and fennel seeds.

PORKVINDALU

What you'll need

Portions – 6
Pork Belly – 690gms (trimmed and cut into small cubes)
Pork leg – 740gms (trimmed and cut into small cubes)
Water – 1300ml
Whole red Kashmiri chilli – 40gms
Mustard seeds – 10gms
Cumin seeds – 10gms
Coriander seeds – 10gms
Green cardamom – 2pcs
Cinnamon – 2gms
Ginger – 20gms
Garlic – 20gms
Cloves – 2gms

Peppercorns – 2gms
Whole grain mustard – 25gms
Kashmiri chilli powder – 10gms
Malt vinegar – 125ml
Water (lukewarm) – 125ml

Oil – 50ml
Red onions – 200gms
Ginger garlic paste – 30gms (base recipe)
Tomato paste – 50gms
Tomato puree – 125gms
Salt – 12gms
Madras onions/Shallots – 75gms
Balsamic Vinegar – 50ml
Sugar – 10gms

How it's done

1. Soak the Kashmiri red chilli, mustard seeds, cumin seeds, coriander seeds, green cardamom, cinnamon, ginger, garlic, mustard, Kashmiri red chilli powder, peppercorns, cloves, malt vinegar and wholegrain mustard in lukewarm water overnight and then grind to a fine paste.
2. Soak the shallots in the balsamic vinegar.
3. Chop the red onions.
4. Heat oil in a pan, add red onions and sauté until golden brown, which should take 5-7 minutes.
5. Add ginger and garlic paste and cook for a couple of minutes. Add the salt, then the tomato purée and tomato paste and stir constantly, adding (300 ml) of water. Simmer for two minutes.
6. Now add the ground paste and saute it for five minutes on a low heat. Add the pork cubes and again saute on a low heat for 5-7 minutes.
7. Stir constantly until the masala coats the pork. Now add the water (1000ml) and give it a good boil. Once the curry starts boiling cover it with a lid and simmer for approximately an hour. Check the pork cubes are cooked then take off the heat.
8. In a separate pan place the soaked shallots and balsamic vinegar mixture with sugar and make a reduction. Once the shallots are coated with the balsamic reduction add to the cooked pork curry. This is delicious served a day later because the pork takes on the extra flavours of the pickling spicy sauce.

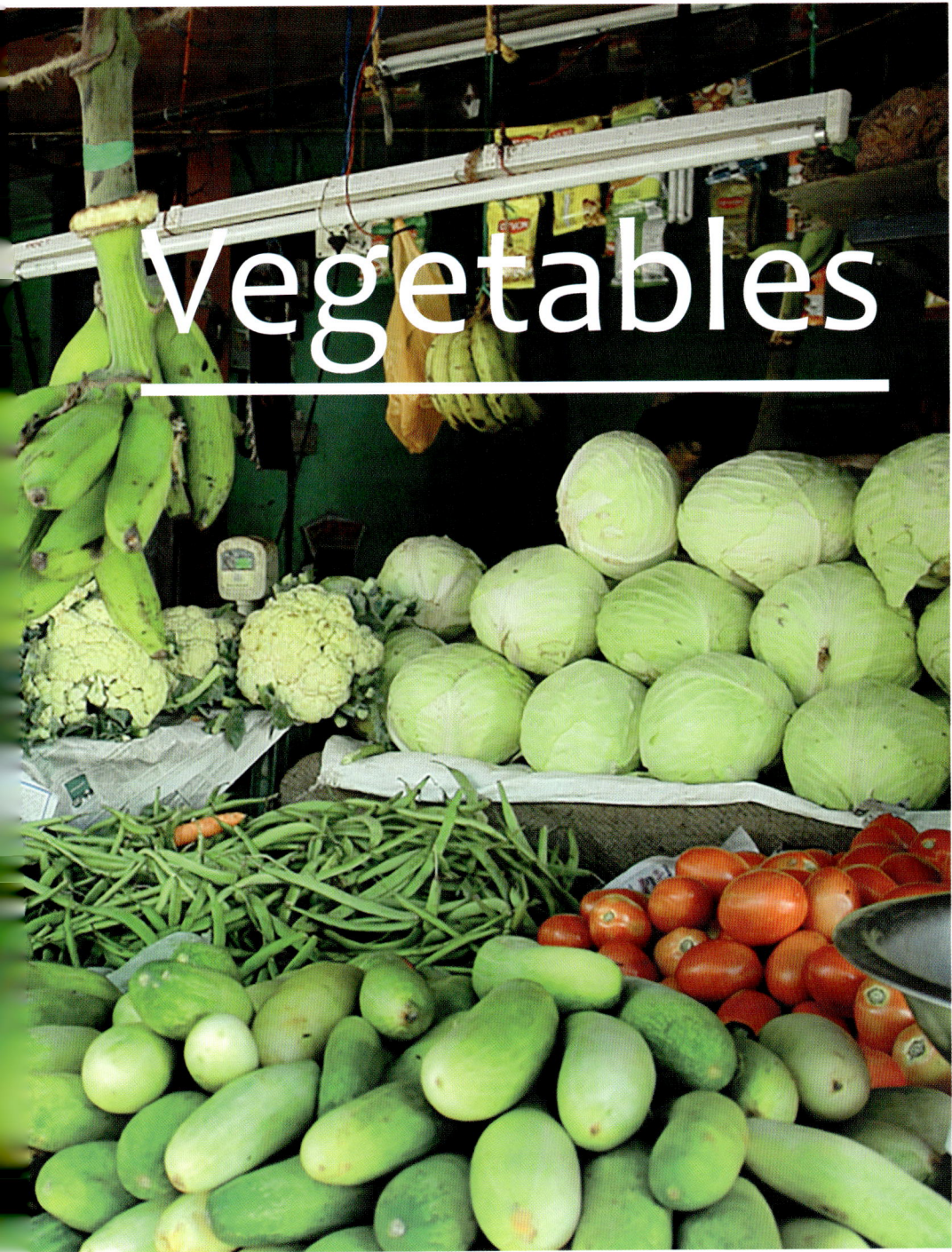

Vegetables

SAAG KHUMB

What you'll need

Portion – 4
Onions chopped – 250gms
Oil – 60ml
Green cardamom – 3 pieces
Cumin seeds– 2gms
Bay leaves – 2pieces
Tomato chopped– 100gms
Ginger garlic paste – 12gms
Salt – 10gms
Kashmiri chilli powder – 10gms
Turmeric powder – 2gms

Coriander powder – 6gms
Mushrooms – 200gms
Chopped & blanched spinach leaves – 300gms
Single cream – 100ml
Butter – 40gms
Kasoori methi leaves – 2gms
Crushed black peppercorns – 2gms
Chana masala powder – 2gms

How it's done

1. Wash the mushrooms and cut into small pieces then chop the onions and tomatoes.
2. Heat some oil in a pan, add the cumin seeds and allow them to crackle; then add in the green cardamom and bay leaves.
3. Once the spices crackle add in the chopped onions and cook until light brown then mix in the ginger garlic paste. Fry for a couple of minutes, lower the heat and add in the turmeric powder, Kashmiri chilli powder, coriander powder and salt. Stir for a minute and add in the tomatoes.
4. Leave to cook and once the masala mixture starts oozing with oil, mix in the mushrooms and cook them for a few minutes then add the chopped, blanched spinach and cook for another 5 minutes.
5. Finally add the butter and finish with kasoori methi leaves, crushed black peppercorns, chana masala powder and cream. Serve hot.

DALTADKA

What you'll need

Portion – 6
Chana dal – 75gms
Toor dal – 75gms
Moong dal – 75gms
Masoor dal – 75gms
Water – 1.5 litres
Turmeric powder – 2gms
Salt – 12 gms
Oil – 25ml

STIR FRY
Oil – 50ml
Cumin seeds – 4gms
Onions – 200gms
Tomato – 100gms
Chopped ginger – 10gms
Green chilli chopped – 4gms

TEMPERING
Oil – 25ml
Chopped garlic – 10gms
Kashmiri chilli powder – 1gm
Coriander leaves – 10gms

How it's done

1. Mix the lentils using 75gms each of chana, masoor, toor and moong dal. Wash them then add to a thick-bottomed pan with 1.5 litres of water. Add turmeric, salt and oil and bring to boil. Skim any impurities from the top. Simmer until the lentils are cooked al-dante (firm to bite). Remove from the heat.
2. Chop the garlic, ginger, green chilli, onions, tomatoes and fresh coriander leaves.
3. Heat the oil in a separate pan. Add the cumin seeds and allow them to crackle. Then add the ginger and green chilli and stir fry it until it turns golden brown. Now add the onions and saute for few minutes until the onions starts turning light brown, followed by tomatoes and cook both of them to form a masala mixture. Add it back to the cooked lentils and bring to boil, and keep aside.
4. For the final tempering, heat the oil in a separate pan and brown the chopped garlic. Take off the heat, add the Kashmiri chilli powder and add it to cooked dal.
5. Finish it with fine chopped coriander.
6. Serve hot.

PUNJABI CHANA MASALA

What you'll need

Portion – 4
Chickpeas – 200gms
Water – 2.5 litre
Baking Soda – 1gm
Tea bag – 2 piece
Salt – 10gms

Masala:
Oil – 50ml
Cumin seeds – 5gms
Sliced onions – 400gms
Ginger garlic paste – 30gms
Coriander powder – 6gms
Chat masala – 2gms
Amchur powder – 2gms
Chana masala powder – 6gms
Kasoori methi leaves powder – 2gms
Kashmiri chilli powder – 1gm
Tomato puree – 50gms
Demerara sugar – 10gms
Turmeric powder – 2gms

How it's done

1. Soak the chickpeas in 2.5 litres of water with the tea bags for at least 12 hours. In a pan add the soaked chickpeas with the teabags along with salt and baking soda. Boil it for an hour until the chickpeas are cooked.
2. Heat the oil in a separate pan. Add cumin seeds and allow them to crackle. Add sliced onions and cook until browned. Add the ginger garlic paste and stir for a couple of minutes until browned. Lower the heat and add coriander powder, chat masala powder, amchur powder, chana masala powder, kasoori methi powder, turmeric powder and Kashmiri chilli powder. Stir for a minute then add the tomato puree. Mix all the spices together.
3. Remove the tea bags from the chickpeas. Add the chickpea mixture to the spices and bring to the boil. Simmer for at least half an hour, until the masala paste coats the chickpeas. Add the sugar, check the seasoning and serve hot.

SAVOY CABBAGE CARROT AND RUNNER BEAN THORAN

What you'll need

Portion – 6
Savoy cabbage – 300gms
Carrot – 150gms (peeled and julienne)
Runner beans – 150gms (string removed and thin julienne)
Red onion chopped – 80gms
Coconut oil/vegetable oil – 50ml
Urad dal split – 12gms
Mustard seeds – 5gms
Curry leaves – 3gms
Green chilli chopped – 8gms
Salt – 8gms
Whole red chilli(chopped) – 2gms
Ginger chopped – 8gms
Coconut grated fresh – 300gms
Turmeric powder – 3gms

How it's done

1. Remove damaged outer leaves, cut the cabbage in quarters over a stable cutting board. Remove the white core and julienne the cabbage finely.
2. Heat oil in a wok for the stir fry and add split urad dal. Allow to turn golden brown.
3. Now add the mustard seeds and allow to crackle.
4. Then add green chilli, ginger, curry leaves, red onions, and red chilli. Stir for a minute.
5. Now add grated coconut, turmeric powder and salt. Stir constantly.
6. Now add the carrot and runner beans and saute for a couple of minutes until the runner beans are just done but still have bite.
7. Add the savoy cabbage and stir for 2-3 minutes. Check the seasoning and serve hot.

PANEER KOFTA
MAKHANI

What you'll need

Portion – 6
Paneer (Indian cottage cheese) – 500gms
Grated potato – 150gms (base recipe)
Green chilli chopped – 2gms
Ginger chopped – 5gms
Salt – 4gms
Chat masala – 4gms
Coriander leaves chopped – 8gms
Cumin powder – 2gms
Oil to fry
Makhani sauce – 1200 gms (base recipe)

How it's done

1. Grate the paneer finely. In a bowl combine the paneer, grated potato, green chilli, ginger chopped, salt, chat masala and coriander leaves. Knead the ingredients together to make a dough, and divide the dough into 18 balls of 35gms each, shape it like a ball and deep fry in oil at 180C for 2-3 minutes, rest a minute in between and keep aside.
2. In a pan, reheat the makhani sauce. Once the sauce starts bubbling add the fried koftas. Check the seasoning and serve hot. Serve three koftas per portion.

POTATO

What you'll need

Portion – 4
Baby Potatoes – 900gms (peeled with the big ones cut into two)
Turmeric – 1gm
Salt – 10gms

Onions chopped – 300gms
Ginger chopped – 10gms
Green chilli chopped – 8gms
Urad dal split – 4gms
Mustard seeds – 2gms
Curry leaves – 2gms
Turmeric powder – 1gm
Salt – 8gms
Cumin powder – 2gms
Red chilli whole – 4gms (crushed with hand)
Vegetable oil – 50ml
Coriander leaves chopped – 5gms

How it's done

1. In thick-bottom pan add the potatoes with turmeric and salt. Cover with water and bring it to the boil. Cook the potatoes, which should take 6 - 8 minutes. Strain in a colander.
2. Heat the oil in a non-stick pan. Add urad dal and allow it to brown. Then add the mustard seeds and allow them to crackle. Add the ginger, green chilli, curry leaves, red chilli and onions and sauté for couple of minutes until the onions become translucent.
3. Now add the salt, turmeric powder, boiled potatoes and combine. Sprinkle the cumin powder on top and toss for a couple of minutes until the potatoes get a nice crust. Add the chopped coriander leaves, check the seasoning and serve hot.

PANEER CHATPATA

What you'll need

Portion – 5
Chatpata sauce – 1000gms (base recipe)
Paneer – 600gms
Bell pepper, red – 1 piece
Bell pepper, green – 1 piece
Bell pepper, yellow – 1 piece
Coriander leaves chopped – 20gms
Kadai masala powder – 20gms (base recipe)
Kasoori methi leaves – 4gms
Oil – to fry paneer

How it's done

1. Cut the paneer into batons of 30gm each, giving you 20 pieces. Deep fry in hot oil for 2-3 minutes. Take off the oil and leave it in water to soften.
2. Remove the core of the bell peppers and cut into thick batons.
3. In a thick-bottomed pan heat the chatpata sauce. Loosen the sauce with 200ml of water. Once the sauce starts bubbling add the paneer and bell pepper batons. Stir fry for another 3-4 minutes. Now sprinkle on the kadai masala powder, coriander leaves, kasoori methi leaves. Make sure the masala coats the paneer and the peppers. Check the seasoning and serve hot.

RICE

Pilaf Rice

What you'll need

Portion – 5
Basmati Rice – 500gms
Pure butter ghee – 50gms
Cumin seeds – 1gm
Green cardamom – 1gm

Cinnamon – 1gm
Cloves – 1gm
Bayleaf – 1gm
Salt – 8gms
Water – 800ml

How it's done

1. Wash the rice couple of times to remove any dirt and dust. Soak the basmati rice in water for one-and-a-half hours. Drain in a colander.
2. In a thick-bottomed pan, heat the butter ghee and add the cumin seeds. Allow them to pop. Now add the cinnamon, green cardamom and cloves and allow the spices to release their flavour without burning. Add 800 ml of water along with salt and bring to boil.
3. Now add the rice to the boiling water and allow it to cook. Once the water evaporates and the rice is visible, lower the heat and cover it with a lid. Allow the rice to cook on a low heat for another 8-10 minutes.
4. Remove the pan from the heat. Keep the lid on for another 8-10 minutes. Open the rice, without breaking the grains. Serve hot.

Steamed Rice

What you'll need

Portion – 4
Basmati rice – 300gms
Oil – 30ml
Cloves – 4pieces
Salt – 16gms
Water – 1.5 litres

How it's done

1. Wash and soak the basmati rice for an hour then drain the water in a colander.
2. Bring the water to the boil along with the cloves and oil. Once it starts boiling add the drained rice. Allow the rice to cook, which should take between 8 and 10 minutes. Once the rice is just done add the salt and drain it in a colander. After a couple of minutes, fork through the rice without breaking the grains to release any trapped steam.

Coconut Rice

What you'll need

Portion – 5
Basmati rice – 300gms
Oil – 30ml
Cloves – 4pieces
Salt – 16gms
Water – 1.5 litres

TEMPERING
Oil – 25ml
Urad dal, split – 10gms
Chopped ginger – 10gms
Mustard seeds – 5gms
Chopped whole dry red chilli – 5gms
Desiccated coconut – 150gms (medium)
Chopped curry leaves – 5gms

How it's done

1. Wash and soak the basmati rice for an hour then drain the water in a colander.
2. Bring the water to the boil along with the cloves and oil. Once it starts boiling add the drained rice. Once the rice is just done add the salt and drain it in a colander. After a couple of minutes, fork through the rice without breaking the grains to release any trapped steam.
3. Heat oil in a pan and add urad dal. Allow it to turn brown, then place the mustard seeds in the pan and allow to crackle. Then add the chopped ginger, red chilli and curry leaves and stir for a minute. Now add the desiccated coconut and stir further for a couple of minutes without browning the coconut,. Combine the rice without breaking the grains. Mix well and serve hot.

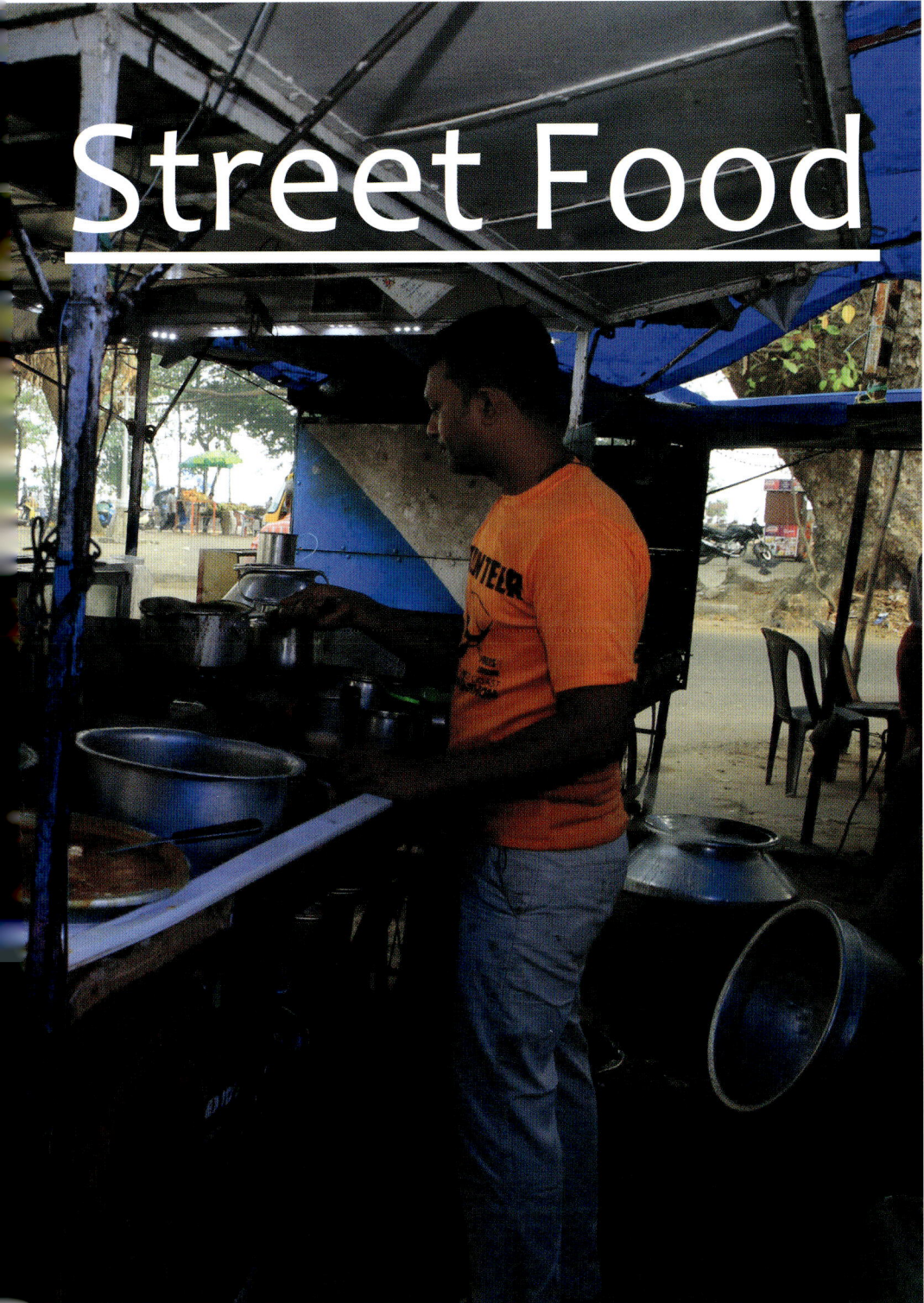

Street Food

BOMBAY FRANKIE ROLL
– BEEF

What you'll need

Portion – 16
Beef (top rump) – 1kg
Onions – 200gms
Ginger garlic paste – 30gms
Tomato – 20gms
Green chilli – 8gms
Kashmiri chilli powder – 10gms
Turmeric powder – 2gms
Coriander powder – 10gms
Salt – 8gms
Cloves – 1gm
Cinnamon – 2gms
Bay leaf – 3piece
Green cardamom – 1gm

How it's done

1. In a blender, place the onions, tomatoes, ginger garlic paste, green chilli, Kashmiri chilli powder, turmeric powder and coriander powder and grind to a fine paste.
2. In an oven-proof pan with a lid, add the beef rump and pour the ground paste over the top then marinade for 12 hours or longer for the best flavour.
3. Once the beef is marinated add the salt, cloves, cinnamon, bay leaf and green cardamom along with 2 litres of water. The water should cover the beef. Now put the lid on and cook in the oven at 120C for approximately four-and-a-half to five hours. Take the beef from the cooked water. Allow to cool. Pull the beef and keep aside. Meanwhile strain the cooked beef water with a fine sieve and use the water in the onion masala.

Onion Masala

What you'll need

Vegetable oil – 100ml
Onions sliced – 2kg
Salt – 10gms
Cooked water – 500ml

How it's done

1. In a thick-bottomed pan heat, add the oil and cook the sliced onions with salt on a low heat.
2. Add the cooking water little by little and cook the onions for at least 40-50 minutes, until they turn dark brown and are reduced by half.

Tempering

Vegetable oil – 50ml
Coconut chips – 80gms
Garlic sliced – 50gms
Ginger julienne – 60gms
Curry leaves – 3gms

1. In a separate pan, heat the oil and add the coconut chips. Allow them to turn light brown then add the sliced garlic and ginger julienne. Cook for another 2-3 minutes until they are golden brown. Now add the curry leaves and add the tempering to the onion masala.
2. Crushed peppercorns – 10gms
3. Heat the onion masala and add the pulled beef and finish with crushed peppercorns and keep aside.
4. Divide the pulled beef mixture into 16 x 100gm portions.

To assemble

Eggs – 16
Pickled red onion (base recipe)
Pickled cucumber (base recipe)
Green chutney (base recipe)
Lettuce, sliced
Oil
Chappati – 16 pieces (base recipe)

1. Beat the eggs. Pour oil into a pan followed by one ladle of egg. Spread the eggs evenly in the pan. Now place the cooked chappati on the egg omellete. Turn the chappati over and keep aside.
2. To assemble each Frankie, in silver foil place the chappati, egg-omellete-side-up. Place the pulled beef mixture (100gms) and roll it once. Now add the pickled red onion, cucumber, lettuce and the green chutney. Now close the sides and wrap it tightly.
3. Serve with green chutney.

BOMBAYFRANKIEROLL
– CHICKEN

What you'll need

Portion – 10
Chicken tikka red marination – 800gms (base recipe)
Chatpata sauce – 600gms from base recipe
Chappati – 10 pieces (base recipe)
Eggs – 10
Pickled red onion (base recipe)
Pickled cucumber (base recipe)
Green chutney (base recipe)
Lettuce, sliced
Oil

How it's done

1. Cook the chicken tikka as mentioned in base recipe, once cooked cut each tikka into long slices.
2. Heat chatpata sauce in pan, add the cooked chicken tikka stir fry well, without breaking the tikka pieces. This portion is enough to make fillings for 10 Frankie rolls.
3. Beat the eggs. Pour oil into a pan followed by one ladle of egg. Spread the eggs evenly in the pan. Now place the cooked chappati on the egg omellete. Turn the chappati over and keep aside.
4. Place the chicken tikka mixture inside (100gms) the chap pati and roll it once. Now add the pickled red onion, cucumber, lettuce and the green chutney. Close the sides and wrap it tightly.
5. Serve with green chutney.

VADAPAO

What you'll need

Portion – 6

Vada (potato dumpling):
Grated potato – 400gms (base recipe)
Vegetable oil – 25ml
Urad dal split – 4gms
Mustard seeds – 2gms
Ginger chopped – 4gms
Green chilli chopped – 6gms
Turmeric powder – 2gms
Salt – 2gms
Curry leaves chopped – 2gms
Onions chopped – 50gms

Batter:
Gram flour – 150gms
Water – 150ml
Bicarbonate of soda – 1gm
Turmeric powder – 2gms
Salt – 2gms
Oil to deep fry

Pao – 6 (base recipe)
Butter
Ghati powder (base recipe)
Green chutney (base recipe)
Tamarind chutney (base recipe)
Salad leaves (base recipe)
Whole green chilli – 6
Rock salt – to sprinkle

How it's done

1. Heat oil in a pan. Add urad dal and allow it to turn golden brown. Then add mustard seeds and allow them to crackle, followed by ginger, green chilli, curry leaves and onions. Sauté for a couple of minutes then add the the turmeric powder, salt and add grated potatoes. Mix well and take off the heat. Allow to cool down and divide the mixture into 6x 70gms balls.
2. In a bowl whisk the above ingredients to form a batter and leave for 5 – 10 minutes.
3. Pre heat the oil to 160C and dip the potato balls in the batter. Add one by one to the oil and fry for 3- 4 minutes.
4. Fry the green chilli in hot oil for couple of seconds, take off the oil and sprinkle it with rock salt.

To serve

1. Cut the pao in half and toast it in a pan with butter. Then apply green chutney on one side and tamarind chutney on the other. Sprinkle ghati powder on both of them and sandwich the vada in between as shown in the picture with mixed salad leaves along with pickled red onion and cucumber. The green chilli with salt should be served to the side.

KERALASTYLEFRIED
CHICKEN

What you'll need

Portion – 5
Chicken thighs – 1.2 kgs (approximately 10pcs)
Ginger chopped – 15gms
Green chilli chopped – 4gms
Kashmiri chilli powder – 15gms
Turmeric powder – 2gms
Salt – 8gms
Lemon juice – 30ml
Fennel seeds crushed – 2gms
Coriander seeds crushed – 5gms
Ginger garlic paste – 22gms
Curry leaves chopped – 2gms
Rice flour coarse – 25gms
Batter flour – 25gms (base recipe)
Oil – to fry

How it's done

1. Trim the fat from the thighs and cut each one into 2 pieces.
2. In a bowl marinate the chicken thighs with ginger, green chilli, Kashmiri chilli powder, turmeric powder, salt, lemon juice, curry leaves and ginger garlic paste. Mix well. Now add the coriander and fennel seeds, rice flour and batter flour.
3. Pre heat the fryer to 170C and fry the chicken thighs for 2 minutes. Now rest for 1 minute and then fry the chicken again for another 2 minutes. Rest for a further minute and then fry for another 3 minutes. Rest for a minute before serving.
4. Serve with: Green chutney (base recipe); Salad leaves (base recipe); Pickled red onion (base recipe); Pickled cucumber (base recipe).

VENISON PAO

What you'll need

Portion – 6
Vegetable oil – 75ml
Venison mince – 500gms
Fennel seeds – 3gms
Onions, sliced – 500gms
Salt – 8gms
Crushed black peppercorns – 5gms
Turmeric powder – 2gms
Kashmiri chilli powder – 3gms
Coriander powder – 5gms
Ginger garlic paste – 15gms

Fennel powder – 2gms
Tomato puree – 50gms
Water – 500ml
Pao – 6 (base recipe)
Eggs – 6
Oil
Butter
Salad leaves (base recipe)
Pickled red onion (base recipe)
Pickled cucumber (base recipe)

How it's done

1. Heat the oil in a thick-bottomed pan. Add the sliced onion and cook for 15 minutes until lightly golden brown.
2. Add the venison mince and fennel seeds and braise for further 3- 4 minutes.
3. Add the ginger garlic paste and cook until the raw smell disappears and the mix starts catching the bottom of the pan.
4. Now lower the heat and add the turmeric powder, coriander powder, Kashmiri chilli powder and salt. Stir for minute without burning the powdered spices. Add the tomato puree and cook further.
5. Add the water, with 300ml initially. Bring it to the boil then cover it with a lid and simmer for 12-15 minutes.
6. Check the venison again and add another 200ml of water. Simmer for another 10-12 minutes.
7. Once the venison mince is cooked, sprinkle with fennel powder and crushed black peppercorns. Check the seasoning.
8. Divide the mixture into 100gms and per portion and serve with one egg.
9. In a pan, fry the eggs and keep them sunny side up. Cut the brioche in half and brush with melted butter. Toast it in a pan. Place the venison mince on the brioche and top it with fried eggs.
10. Serve with mixed salad leaves along with pickled red onion and cucumber.

Desserts

PISTACHIO ICE-CREAM

What you'll need

Portion – 2 Pacojet containers
Egg yolk – 200gms
Sugar – 200gms
Pistachio – 200gms
Double cream – 300ml
Milk – 300ml
Glucose – 120gms

How it's done

1. Boil double cream, milk and glucose.
2. Beat the egg yolk and sugar. Add the cooked double cream mixture, pass through a sieve and allow it to cool. Transfer into two Pacojet containers, adding 100gms of pistachio into each container and freeze for at least 24 hours.
3. Churn the sorbet in the Pacojet. One container will give 15 scoops of ice-cream.

CHOCOMOSA

What you'll need

Portion – 4
Flaked almonds – 10gms
Callebaut Dark Chocolate
Callets 53.8% – 75gms
Butter unsalted – 30gms
Caster sugar – 12gms
Egg medium – 1
Spring roll pastry pouch – 8
(base recipe)
Oil (for frying)
Plain flour-handful
Banana
Sugar

How it's done

1. Preheat the oven to 220C and the roast the almonds for 5 minutes until toasted but not burned.
2. Melt the chocolate, butter, sugar and egg in a bain-marie, mixing gently occasionally, until it forms a smooth ganache. It should take about 7 minutes. Leave to cool, then add the roasted almond fakes. Mix well and refrigerate for 12 hours.
3. Divide the ganache into 8 equal parts.
4. Mix some flour with water to make a paste to stick the edges of the samosa together, which will stop the ganache from oozing out when gently frying.
5. Place one spoon of ganache into the pastry pouch, continue folding into a samosa shape, enclosing the ganache mixture. Stick the sides well with the flour paste.
6. Deep fry at 180C for 30 seconds.
7. Slice the banana, dust with sugar and caramelize with a blow torch.
8. To serve place two slices of banana, with the chocomosa on top with vanilla ice-cream (See Page 216)

COCONUTWATERAND
MALIBUSORBET

What you'll need

Portion – 2 Pacojet containers
Sugar – 120gms
Coconut water – 1400ml
Glucose – 100gms
Malibu – 200ml

How it's done

1. In a pan boil the sugar, coconut water, glucose and Malibu. Once the sugar melts take it off the heat and allow it to cool. Transfer it into two Pacojet containers and freeze it for at least 24 hours. Churn the sorbet in the Pacojet. One container will give 15 scoops of sorbet.

PASSIONFRUITAND CHILLISORBET

What you'll need

Portion – 2 Pacojet containers
Demerara sugar – 100gms
Glucose – 120gms
Water – 100ml

Passion fruit puree – 800ml
Mango pulp – 200ml
Fresh red chilli chopped – 2gms
Chopped ginger – 2gms

How it's done

1. In a pan, boil the sugar and glucose along with the water until the sugar has dissolved. Take off the heat and allow to cool.
2. Mix the other ingredients with the cooked sugar syrup and freeze for at least 24 hours. Churn the sorbet in the Pacojet. One container will give 15 scoops of sorbet.

ROSEPETALICE-CREAM

What you'll need

Portion – 2 Pacojet containers
Glucose – 120gm
Milk – 200ml
Double cream – 400ml
Egg yolks – 200gm
Sugar – 150gms
Rose syrup – 60ml
Rose petal dry – two handfuls
Fresh rose petal – two handfuls

How it's done

1. Boil the double cream and glucose along with the dry rose petals.
2. Beat the egg yolk with the sugar.
3. Mix both together and allow to cool down. Once cooled add the rose syrup and divide the mixture into two Pacojet containers. Place one handful of fresh rose petals into each container and freeze for at least 24 hours. Churn the ice-cream in the Pacojet. One container will give 15 scoops of ice-cream.

TANDOORI PINEAPPLE

What you'll need

Portion – 4
Pineapple whole – 1160gms (1 piece)
Bhuno besan – 10gms (gram flour roux/base recipe)
Cardamom powder – 2gms
Nutmeg powder – a pinch
Saffron powder – a pinch
Single cream – 30ml
Honey – 60gms

How it's done

1. Top and tail the pineapple, remove the skin and cut into quarters, lengthways. Remove the hard core and cut the soft flesh into 40-45gms chunks, giving 12 pieces of pineapple.
2. In a blender combine all the ingredients, except the pineapple. Blend and pass through a fine sieve. Marinate the pineapple in the mixture for 3 hours.
3. Finally place the pineapple on the skewers and cook in the tandoor oven. Alternatively, pre-heat an oven to 180C and bake the pineapple for 5 minutes. Serve hot with 3 pieces per portion with coconut ice-cream (See Page 216).

ROSE CREME BRULEE

What you'll need

Portion – 9 x 60ml portions
Double cream – 360ml
Milk – 120ml
Demerara sugar– 30gms
Egg yolks – 85gms
Rose syrup – 70ml
Rose petals, dried – 2gms

How it's done

1. Boil the double cream and milk together.
2. With a whisk, mix the sugar and egg yolk together. Add in the boiled double cream, milk and rose syrup. Combine well and pass through a fine sieve.
3. Add the dried rose petals to the mixture. Combine well and portion into ramekins.
4. Preheat the oven to 250C. In a double boiler, place the ramekins and cover with silver foil. Cook for 30 minutes. Once done take off the double boiler to cool down and then keep refrigerated.

Garam Masala Crème Brulee

What you'll need

Portion – 8 x 60ml
Double cream – 360ml
Milk – 120ml
Demerara sugar – 40gms
Egg yolks – 85gms
Garam masala powder – 2gms

How it's done

1. Boil the double cream and milk together. With a whisk, mix the sugar and egg yolk together. Add in the boiled double cream and milk. Combine well and pass through a fine sieve.
2. Add the garam masala powder to the mixture. Combine well and portion into ramekins.
3. Preheat the oven to 250C. In a double boiler, place the ramekins and cover with silver foil and cook for 30 minutes. Once done take off the double boiler to cool down and then keep refrigerated.

Garam Masala Powder

Mace – 4gms
Green cardamom – 5gms
Star anise – 4gms
Cloves – 3gms
Cinnamon – 6gms

1. Dry roast the above ingredients on a low heat and grind to fine powder. It will give a yield of 20gms. Store in an air tight container.

To Serve

1. When ready to serve, wipe round the top edge of the dishes. Sprinkle caster sugar over each ramekin then use a blow torch to caramelize it. Hold the flame just above the sugar and keep moving it round and round until caramelized.
2. Serve one rose petal and garam masala crème brulee per portion.

COCONUT ICE-CREAM

What you'll need

Egg yolk – 75gms
Sugar – 75gms
Coconut milk powder – 75gms
Double cream – 150ml
Milk – 150ml

How it's done

1. Boil the double cream and milk. Take off the heat and mix with coconut milk powder.
2. Beat the egg yolk and sugar. Add the cooked double cream mixture. Pass through a sieve and allow to cool. Transfer into one Pacojet container. Freeze for at least 24 hours. Churn the ice-cream in the Pacojet. One container will give 15 scoops of coconut ice-cream.

Vanilla Ice-cream

What you'll need

Milk – 250ml
Double cream – 250ml
Egg yolk – 80gms
Sugar – 80gms
Vanilla – 1 pod

How it's done

1. Boil the milk and double cream along with the vanilla pod. Beat the egg yolk and sugar. Mix with the cooked milk. Allow to cool down and pass through a fine sieve. Transfer into a Pacojet container. Freeze for at least 24 hours
2. Churn the ice-cream in the Pacojet. One container will give 15 scoops of vanilla ice-cream.

Base Recipes

Chatpata Sauce

Yield is 1200gms

Oil – 100ml
Onions chopped – 1kg
Cumin seeds – 4gms
Turmeric powder – 5gms
Coriander powder – 5gms
Kashmiri chilly powder – 5gms
Salt – 10gms
Ginger garlic paste – 35gms
Ginger chopped – 15gms
Garlic chopped – 10gms
Green chilli chopped – 6gms
Kasoori methi leaves – 1gm
Kitchen king powder – 5gms
Tomato puree – 500gms

1. Heat the oil in a thick-bottomed pan. Add cumin seeds and allow them to crackle. Now add the chopped garlic, ginger and green chilli and allow to turn slightly brown. Now add the onions and sauté the for at least half an hour until they are soft but not browned. Now add the ginger garlic paste and cook for a further 5-7 minutes.
2. Lower the heat and add the turmeric powder, coriander powder, Kashmiri chilli powder, kitchen king powder and salt and stir for a couple of minutes.
3. Now add the tomato puree and cook for another half an hour until the onion and tomatoes are cooked and form a masala paste texture. Sprinkle in kasoori methi leaves, check the seasoning and keep aside.
4. Once cooled keep in an air tight container and refrigerate.

Makhani Sauce

Yield is 1300gms

Tomato Puree – 1kg
Water – 200ml & 700ml
Milk powder – 15gms
Salt – 10gms
Butter – 2 x 60gms
Cloves – 1gm
Green cardamom – 1gm
Mace – 1gm
Cinnamon – 2gms
Bay leaf – 3 piece
Ginger garlic paste – 30gms
Kashmiri chilli powder – 4gms
Coriander powder – 8gms
Kitchen King – 5gms
Cashew nuts – 60gms
Oil to fry

1. In a thick bottom pan, place tomato puree, milk powder, salt, butter, water and cook for half an hour until the tomatoes are cooked.
2. Fry the cashew nuts in oil until light brown. Make a paste with 200ml of water.
3. In a separate pan melt the butter on a low heat. Add the cloves, green cardamom, mace, cinnamon, bay leaf and ginger garlic paste. Once the ginger garlic paste starts browning and catches the bottom of the pan add the Kashmiri chilli powder, coriander powder, Kitchen King and stir for a minute on a slow fire.
4. Now add the cashew nut paste and keep on stirring on a low heat for up to 10 minutes. Now add the cooked tomato mixture and 700ml of water. Cook for another half an hour. Once cooked, pass the mixture through a sieve.
5. Bring the sauce bring to the boil in a pan and finish it with: Single cream – 200ml; Sugar – 40gms; kasoori methi leaves – 5gms.

6. Once cooled keep in an air-tight container and refrigerate.

Mint Chutney

Yield is 355gms

Coriander leaves – 200gms (stem removed and washed)
Mint leaves – 35gms (pick the leaves, washed)
Green chilli – 2gms
Garlic – 7gms
Hung yoghurt – 50gms
Sugar – 15gms
Salt – 8gms

1. Drain the washed coriander and mint in a colander for few minutes to remove the water. Place the mint, coriander leaves, green chilli, garlic , hung yoghurt, sugar and salt in a food processor and blend to a chutney. Don't blend again and again otherwise the mint chutney will lose its green colour. Empty into a container and keep it refrigerated.

Basil Paste

Yield is 65gms

Basil leaves – 60gms (stem removed)
Oil – 25ml

1. Grind to a fine paste with oil.
2. Keep refrigerated.

Punjabi Chana Masala

Yield is 900-1000gms

Chickpeas – 200gms
Water – 2.5 litre
Baking soda – 1gm
Tea bag – 2
Salt – 10gms

Masala:
Oil – 50ml
Cumin seeds – 5gms
Sliced onions – 400gms
Ginger garlic paste – 30gms
Coriander powder – 6gms
Chat masala – 2gms
Amchur powder – 2gms
Chana masala powder – 6gms
Kasoori methi leaves powder – 2gms
Kashmiri chilli powder – 1gm
Tomato puree – 50gms
Demerara sugar – 10gms
Turmeric powder – 2gms

1. Soak the chickpeas in 2.5 litres of water with the tea bags for at least 12 hours. In a pan add the soaked chickpeas with the tea bag plus salt and baking soda. Boil for an hour until the chickpeas are cooked.
2. Heat the oil, add the cumin seeds and allow them to crackle. Add the sliced onions and cook until browned. Add the ginger garlic paste and stir it for a couple of minutes until browned. Lower the heat then add the coriander powder, chat masala powder, amchur powder, chana masala powder, kasoori methi powder, turmeric powder and Kashmiri chilli powder and stir for a minute. Add the tomato puree and mix all the spices together.
3. Remove the tea bags from the chickpeas. Add the mixture to the spices and bring to boil. Simmer for at least half an hour. Add the sugar, check the consistency and serve hot.
4. Check the seasoning, allow to cool down and keep refrigerated in an airtight container.

Garam Masala Powder – Keralan Style

Yield is 20gms

Fennel seeds – 10gms
Cinnamon – 2gms
Cloves – 2gms
Green cardamom – 6gms

1. Dry roast on a low heat and grind to fine powder then store in an airtight container.

Garam Masala Powder

Yield is 58gms

Cloves – 10gms
Green cardamom – 15gms
Mace – 5gms
Star anise – 5gms
Nutmeg – 6gms
Cinnamon – 20gms
Black cardamom – 5gms
Bayleaf – 1gm

1. Crack the nutmeg and cinnamon into small pieces. Dry roast the spices for a couple of minutes on a low heat. Grind to a fine powder. Pass through a fine sieve and keep it in an airtight container. Store at room temperature.

Chappati – 16

Wheat flour – 750ml
Plain flour – 250ml, plus extra for dusting
Salt – 6gms
Egg – 1
Water – 650ml

1. Sift the flour and salt into a bowl. Add the egg and about two-thirds of the water. Mix until smooth. Slowly add enough of the remaining water to make a soft dough, then turn out on a work surface and knead for a few minutes until smooth and elastic. Return to the bowl and leave to rest for 30 minutes, keeping covered with a damp cloth.
2. Divide the dough into 16 pieces of 100gms each. Shape into a ball and dust with a little flour. Rest for another 20-25 minutes.
3. Flatten each ball with the palms of your hand and then your fingers, pressing out on a floured surface and rolling into 24cm disc with a rolling pin.
4. Heat a flat griddle or a frying pan and place the chappati in it to cook for a few minutes on both sides. Keep aside.

Fried Onion

Yield is 300gms of fried onions

Onions, sliced – 1kg
Oil – 1 litre

1. Heat the oil in a pan. Add half of the onions and fry for 5 minutes, stirring in between, until light golden brown. Lift the fried onions from the oil with a slicer and drain the onion in a colander. Bring the oil back to the heat. Add the rest of the onions and cook the same way.

Chicken Tikka Red Marinade

Yield of cooked chicken tikka is approximately 750gms.

Chicken supreme – 800gms (3pcs)
Trim the chicken breast, cut each one into four pieces, each weighing approximately 65gms

First marinade:
Kashmiri chilli powder – 10gms
Kasoori methi leaves – 2gms
Ginger garlic paste – 20gms
Lemon juice – 10ml
Mustard oil – 15ml
Salt – 3gms

Second marinade:
Hung yoghurt – 150gms
Kashmiri chilli powder – 6gms
Kasoori methi leaves – 1gm
Chana masala powder – 1gm
Ginger garlic paste – 15gms
Mustard oil – 10ml
Salt – 3gms
Amchur powder – 1gm
Chat masala powder – 1gm

1. In a separate bowl mix the chicken pieces with the ingredients from the first marinade and leave for at least 2 hours.
2. In a separate bowl combine the second marinade ingredients and add it to the first marinated chicken. Keep the chicken marinated for at least 2 hours.
3. Pre-heat the oven. Skewer the chicken and cook it in a Tandoor or an oven on a wire rack at 250C for 5 minutes. Now baste with melted butter, lower the temperature to 180C and cook for another 5 minutes. Sprinkle with chat masala and melted butter.

Pear Chutney

Cooked yield is 245gms

Pear – 600gms (4 piece). Remove the eye, and the seeds and slice finely
Green cardamom – 1gm
Cloves – 1gm
Cinnamon – 1gm
Fennel seeds – 2gms
Oil – 25ml
Demerara sugar – 15gms

1. Dry roast the spices on a low heat. In a mortar and pestle, crush until coarse. Remove the outer cover of the cardamom.
2. In thick-bottomed pan heat the oil. Add the crushed spices and sliced pears and cook on a low heat for approximately 55 minutes, stirring in between and making sure it doesn't catch the pan. Allow the pears to cook through until almost mashed
3. Add the Demerara sugar
4. Allow the sugar to melt and coat the pears nicely. It should take approximately 5 minutes. Take off the heat and allow to cool. Store in an air tight container.

Fried Garlic

Yield is 200gms

Garlic chopped – 350gms
Vegetable oil – 300ml

1. Heat oil in a pan, add half of the garlic, 175gms, and fry it for 5 minutes, stirring in between until it turns light golden brown. Drain the garlic in a colander. Bring the oil back to the heat. Add the rest of the garlic and do the same with the remainder.

Tomato Chutney

Yield is 280gms

Tomatoes – 450gms (4 piece)
Oil – 25ml
Asafoetida(hing) – 1gm
Split urad dal – 2gms
Mustard seeds – 2gms
Curry leaves – 1gm
Ginger chopped – 4gms
Green chilli chopped – 1gm
Kashmiri chilli powder –2gms
Turmeric powder– 1gm
Salt – 5gms
Sugar – 5gms
Tomato paste – 40gms
Tomato puree – 60gms

1. Remove the eye of the tomatoes and blanch in hot water for 45 seconds. Peel the skin and discard. Chop the tomatoes into small cubes and keep aside.
2. Heat the oil in a pan. Add urad dal and allow them to brown. Then add the mustard seeds and allow them to crackle. Now add the ginger, green chilli and curry leaves. Lower the heat then add the hing, Kashmiri chilli powder, turmeric powder and chopped tomatoes. Sauté for a minute, then add the salt, sugar, tomato paste and puree. Cook on a low heat for another 25 minutes. Once the tomatoes are mashed and form a consistency finish with: White vinegar – 10ml; Cumin seeds powder – 2gms; Coriander leaves chopped – 4gms
3. Cook for a further 5 minutes, take off the heat and allow to cool. Keep refrigerated.

Coconut, garlic, chilli spice powder (ghati spice)

Yield is 350gms

Desiccated coconut medium – 200gms
Chopped garlic fried – 150gms
Kashmiri chilly powder – 10gms
Chat masala – 4gms
Salt – 4gms

1. In a pan dry roast the desiccated coconut and Kashmiri chilli powder on a low heat for a couple of minutes. Take it off the heat and combine it the with fried garlic, chat masala and salt in a blender. Keep in an air tight container at room temperature.

Hung Yoghurt

Natural yoghurt – 1kg

1. Place it in a muslin cloth and hang it for 90 minutes. After losing the whey the yield will be 735gms. Remove the yoghurt from the cloth and keep refrigerated.

Sweetened Yoghurt

Hung yoghurt – 735 gms
Sugar – 60gms
Salt – 1gm

1. Mix it well with a whisk, not a blender. Keep it in piping bottling for service. The yield will be 795gms, which means you can store it in two piping bottles.

Pickled Beetroot

Beetroot – 490gms (2 pieces)
Rock salt – 35gms
White vinegar – 250ml
Water – 2.5 litre

1. Preheat the oven to 200C. In a steel container, place the beetroot with the rock salt, vinegar and water. Cover it with a lid or silver foil and cook for an hour. Once cooked, drain the water and allow the beetroot to cool down.
2. Now peel the beetroot and slice it finely with a mandolin. With a round cutter, cut into roundels. The beetroot will give about 27 slices.
3. Make a marinade with the following: Oil- 150ml; White vinegar-40ml; Rock salt- 3gms; Crushed black peppercorns-2gms
4. Leave the sliced beetroot in the marinade and keep refrigerated. Use 3 slices per portion.

Kadai Masala Powder

Yield is 40gms

Kashmiri whole dry red chilli – 10gms
Cumin seeds – 10gms
Coriander seeds – 10gms
Black peppercorns – 10gms

1. Dry roast the spices individually on a low heat. In a blender crush the Kashmiri chilli first, then combine the cumin, coriander and black peppercorns and make a coarse spice powder. Store in an airtight container.

Mint Sauce

Yield is 455 gms

Coriander leaves – 135gms (stem removed). Wash the coriander leaves and drain in a colander, otherwise the mint sauce will be too watery and will lose consistency.
Mint leaves – 20gms (pick the leaves and discard the stems)
Green chilli – 2gms
Garlic – 3gms
Hung yoghurt – 40gms

1. Place the above into a blender and grind fast, so not to lose the green colour. Remove it into a bowl and with a whisk mix the following: Hung yoghurt – 200gms; salt – 5gms; sugar – 20gms; mayonnaise – 30gms.
2. Mix it well with a whisk, and keep it in a piping bottle. Keep refrigerated.

Ulli Chutney

Yield is 135gm

Kashmiri whole red chilli – 12gms(4pcs)
Madras onion/shallots – 80gms
White vinegar – 30ml
Salt – 3gms
Coconut oil – 50ml

1. Deseed the Kashmiri chilli. In a blender, coarse grind the madras onions, kashmiri chilli (crush them in a mortar and pestle). Transfer to a bowl and mix with the vinegar, salt and coconut oil. Serve at room temperature.

Tamarind Chutney

Yield is 760gms

Green cardamom – 2gms
Whole dry red chilli – 3gms
Bay leaf – 1 piece
Cinnamon – 1gm
Cumin – 3gms
Fennel seed – 3gms
Salt – 1gm
Black salt – 1gm
Dry ginger powder – 2gms
Black cardamom – 1gm
Kashmiri red chilli – 3gms
Tamarind – 180gms
Jaggery – 540gms
Water – 3200ml

1. Place the above ingredients in a thick-bottomed pan along with the water. Bring to the boil, stirring in between. Simmer for approximately 3 hours. Pass the chutney through a fine sieve. Cool it down and store in a refrigerator.

Passion Fruit and Chilli Dressing

Yield is 430gms

Passion fruit puree – 100gms
Mango pulp – 150gms
Ginger chopped – 1gm
Red chilli chopped – 1gm
Oil – 10ml
Vinegar – 25ml

1. In a bowl mix all the above ingredients with a whisk.
2. Keep Refrigerated.

Red Bell Pepper Sauce

Yield is 330gms

Red bell peppers – 550gms (3 piece)
Oil – 25ml
Garlic chopped – 10gms
Cumin powder – 2gms
Kashmiri chilli powder – 2gms
Salt – 2gms
Mayonnaise – 150gms

1. Cut the bell peppers, remove the core and seeds and chop.
2. Heat the oil in a pan and add the garlic. Cook until light brown add the chopped bell pepper, cumin powder and Kashmiri chilli powder. Keep on cooking for 90 minutes or so then blend to a fine paste. Pass through a fine sieve and keep aside. Allow to cool. Once cooled mix with the mayonnaise.
3. Keep in a piping bottle and refrigerate.

Ginger Garlic Paste

Yield is 325gms

Ginger – 150gms
Garlic peeled – 100gms
Water – 50ml
Oil – 50ml

1. Wash the ginger a couple of times. Slice with the skin on and soak in 50ml of water for 15-20 minutes. Place the ginger in a food processor along with the water and garlic and grind to a fine paste adding oil in between.
2. Keep refrigerated in an airtight container, leave some oil on top.

Mixed Salad Leaves

Leeks – 100gms
Celery – 67gms
Green bell pepper – 1 piece
Red bell pepper – 1 piece
Red cabbage – 20gms
Red raddish small – 54gms (4 piece)
Mustard cress – 3 bunch (30gms)

1. Fine julienne the leek and celery.
2. Peppers: Remove the core and the membrane of the peppers and cut into fine julienne.
3. Remove the thick stalks of the red cabbage and julienne finely.
4. Cut the leaves off the mustard cress.
5. Cut the red raddish into roundels.
6. Mix all together and serve.

Mint Sorbet

Glucose – 120gms
Sugar – 120gms
Water – 525ml
Mint leaves – 50gms
Coriander leaves – 105gms
Whole milk natural yoghurt – 525gms
Garlic – 2gms
Green chilli – 2gms

1. Boil the glucose, sugar and water. Cool it down. Mix it with the yoghurt.
2. Pour the above mixture into two Pacojet containers. Divide the coriander leaves and mint leaves into the containers. Finally, divide the garlic and green chilli into the two containers. Freeze for 24 hours and churn in a Pacojet. One container will yield of 15 scoops of mint sorbet.

Beetroot Pachadi

Yield is 165 gms

Beetroot – 160gms (1piece)
Ginger – 30gms
Coleman's whole grain mustard – 15gms
Hung Yoghurt – 50gms
Oil – 10ml
Salt – 3gms
Cumin powder – 2gms
Single cream – 10ml
Mustard seeds – 2gms

1. Peel the beetroot and fine chop it in a food processor. Peel the ginger and make a smooth paste with 30ml of water in a mixer.
2. Heat the pan. Add the chopped beetroot with salt and cumin powder. Cook until the moisture of the beetroot evaporates. In another pan, heat the oil and add the mustard seeds. Allow it to crackle. Now add the ginger paste and cook it for few minutes until the raw smell of the ginger escapes and it starts catching on the pan. Transfer the cooked ginger paste into the cooked beetroot and cook for a further five minutes.
3. Take the beetroot mixture off the pan and transfer into a mixing bowl. Now add the wholegrain mustard, hung yoghurt, salt and single cream. Mix them well with a spatula. Check the seasoning and keep refrigerated.

Coconut Paste

Yield is 90gms

Desiccated coconut fine – 100gms

1. In a blender grind the coconut to a fine paste. It will take a couple of minutes. Store at room temperature.

Mixed Berry Sauce

Yield will be 680gms

Frozen summer fruits – 1kg (strawberry, redcurrants, raspberry, blackberry, blueberry and cherry)
Nutmeg – 7gms (2 piece, crushed with a rolling pin)
Black peppercorns – 1gm
Cloves – 1gm
White vinegar – 300ml
Sugar – 300gms
Ginger – 30gms (crushed with a rolling pin)

1. Place the above ingredients in a pan and cook on a low heat, stirring in between for approximately 50 minutes. Strain it through a fine sieve and allow to cool.
2. Once cooled mix with: White vinegar-25ml; Oil-10ml
3. Place in 2 piping bottles and keep refrigerated.

Bhuno Besan

Yield is 140gms

Gram flour – 100gms
Vegetable oil – 70ml
Cloves – 3 piece

1. Heat oil in a pan and add gram flour along with cloves. Cook on a low fire, stirring constantly until it turns light brown and nutty. Transfer into a container and allow to cool down. Once cooled, the oil will float on top. Leave it at room temperature.

Red Chilli Paste

Yield is 450gms

Whole Dried Kashmiri Red Chilli – 100gms
Water – 900ml
Oil – 125ml
Water – 125ml

1. In a pan, boil the red chilli with water for approximately 25minutes. Strain the chillies in a colander and discard the cooked water. In a bowl place the chillies and cover with cold water to cool down.
2. After 10-15 minutes, lift the chillies and discard the water and seeds, and put in a blender along with water and oil, adding half first then the rest.
3. Grind to a fine paste, keep in an air tight container and leave some oil on top. Refrigerate or freeze.

Curry Leaf and Garlic Paste (Crab)

Yield is 155gms.

Green chilly – 4gms
Salt – 3gms
Lemon juice – 70ml
Oil – 70ml
Fried garlic – 26gms
Fried curry leaves – 26gms

1. In a blender, grind to a fine paste. Store in a refrigerator.

Boiled, Grated Potatoes

Yield is 900gms

Potatoes, maris piper – 1kg
Water – 2 litre
Salt – 10gms

1. Wash the potatoes thoroughly in running water.
2. Place the potatoes and water in a pan with salt and bring to boil with a lid on for 45 minutes, or until cooked. Drain the water and allow the potatoes to cool down. Once cooled, peel the skin and grate finely. Store in a refrigerator for use.

Samosa Pastry

Portion – 75 pouches

30 sheets of ready made spring roll pastry – 1
(Approx. 250mmx 250mm)

1. Cut the spring roll sheet into 16 five-and-a-half cm rectangles.
2. On the long side of each rectangle, mark 13cm, from the bottom of the left hand corner. Make a cut from this mark to the right hand corner. Take 2 rectangles and put them together at right angles to form an L shape with the joining corner 'cut away'.
3. Fold over each leg to the L once to make a pouch. So each rectangle will make 15 pastry pouches, and a total of 75 pouches from the entire pastry sheet. Add in the samosa mixture and continue folding into a samosa shape, enclosing the mixture.

Pickled – Red Onion and Cucumber

Yield of red onion is 236gms

Yield of cucumber –209gms

Red onion – 285gms (1 piece)
Peel the red onion and slice it
Whole cucumber – 420gms (1 piece)
Cut the cucumber, deseed and slice into thick julienne

Pickling Liquid
Water – 360ml
Vinegar – 240ml
Sugar – 20gms
Salt – 6gms

1. Mix the pickling liquid well and divide into two bowls (300ml each). Soak the cucumber and red onions for 20 minutes, drain and serve, keep refrigerated.

Chick Pea and Potato Mash

Yield is 360gms

Chick pea – 200gms (boiled)
Potatoes – 150gms (boiled and grated)
Vegetable oil – 15ml

1. Combine all together in a blender, keep refrigerated.

Confit Duck Legs

The pulled yield of duck legs is 345gms, per portion 25gms.

Duck legs with skin – 850gms
(210-220gms each 4 pieces)
Cloves – 1gm
Bay leaf – 3 piece
Sea salt – 40gms
Demerara sugar – 18gms
Mace – 2gms
Nutmeg – 2gms
Duck fat/ oil – enough to cover the legs

1. Grind the above spice together, scatter a layer of this mix onto a non-metallic tray and place the duck legs on top skin side down. Sprinkle the remaining spice mix on the top of the duck and leave it for 24 hours in a refrigerator.
2. After 24 hours, preheat the oven to 130C. Rinse the duck legs in cold running water, pat them dry and place them in a flame proof casserole.
3. Cover the legs with duck fat and heat on a hob until the fat reaches 80C on a constant thermometer. Cover the pot and and place it in oven for 2 ½- 3 hours until the duck legs are tender. Remove the pot from the oven and leave the duck to cool down in the pot, covered for 2 hours.
4. When the duck legs are cool, transfer them to a plate and pull the meat and skin. Pass the duck fat through a fine sieve, then transfer them it to a refrigerator and save to use another time.

Pao – Brioche Buns

Plain flour strong – 1kg
Fresh yeast – 25gms
Sugar – 100gms
Milk – 350ml
Eggs – 2
Salt – 15gms
Water – 50ml
Flour to dust
Eggs to brush

1. Mix your dough using a stand mixer. It will be very sticky and have a shaggy appearance. Place a damp kitchen towel directly over the bowl and allow it to rest until it has doubled in size. Depending on how warm your kitchen is, this will take about 1-3 hours. Giving your dough enough time to rise is crucial in bread baking.
2. Once your dough has risen, dump it out onto a lightly floured work surface. Gently flatten or 'punch' down the dough to get rid of any air bubbles. Using a bench scraper, or a chef's knife, cut the dough into 30 pieces of 60gms balls or 60 pieces of 30gm balls. Gently flatten each piece of dough, pull up each side pinching it together in the center. Repeat until the ball is sealed. Flip the ball over, seam side down, and move to an un-floured part of your board: it's easier to roll this way. Place your palm over the top and gently roll into a smooth ball. Transfer each ball onto a parchment lined baking sheet.
3. The dough will need to rise again, the balls should look puffy and slightly risen, about1- 1/2 hrs. When they're ready, gently brush each one with egg wash.
4. Preheat your oven to 180C and place a shallow baking pan on the oven floor. Before the dough goes in, add about 1/2 cup of water to the pan (to create steam). This will help keep the bread nice and moist. Bake for about 12-15 minutes or until golden brown. Transfer to a wire rack to cool completely.

Salad Dressing

Yield is 330gms

English mustard paste – 50gms
Crushed black peppercorns – 5gms
Sugar – 35gms
Chat masala – 5gms
Salt – 3gms
Lemon juice – 175ml
Oil – 120ml

1. Blend the above ingredients together, keep refrigerated.

Flour Mix – Batter

Yield is 168gms

Self raising flour – 30gms
Corn flour – 100gms
Gram flour – 30gms
Chana masala powder – 5gms
Salt – 3gms
Turmeric powder – 1gm

1. Combine all the ingredients together and keep in an air tight container.
2. When needed, mix with enough water to make a batter consistency.

Glossary and Ingredients

Commonly used spices and herbs of cooking

Asafoetida / Hing

This is a dried gum-like resin that is derived from the ferula (giant fennel plants). It is strongly flavoured and bitter and should be used sparingly. As is the case with most spices, its heat pleasantly enhances flavours. Asafoetida is available as a resinous nugget or as a powder mixed with rice flour, which makes it easier to use.

Basmati Rice

With its fragrance and delicate flavour, this variety of rice is used for special occasions. To keep the rice fluffy and to ensure the rice grains do not stick together, wash the rice and soak in cold water before cooking.

Bengali Gram Dal

Another name for channa dal. These split, matt yellow gram lentils are the most widely consumed lentils in India. They are available from Asian food shops. They hold their shape when cooked. You can buy roasted channa dal from Asian food shops. We powder it and add it as a binding agent to recipes like aloo tikki. Yellow split peas make an acceptable substitute, although channa dal has a slightly sweeter, nuttier flavour.

Black Pepper

Pepper in its various forms is one of the most widely used spices in the world. This is the spice that took early spice traders to Kerala, from where it was transported to the rest of the world. Black pepper is the most pungent, both in flavour and aroma. It is used in whole and crushed form.

Black Salt

This traditional condiment in Indian cookery comes from the volcanic mines of northern India and Pakistan. It is valued for its high mineral content but be aware of its sulphurous taste.

Breadcrumbs

Breadcrumbs are bread that has been grated or finely ground, either with or without the crust. Ready-made versions available may also contain coloring, emulsifiers or treatment agents.

Cardamom

These are available as both black and green pods. Ground Cardamom is made from green cardamom pods. Cardamom has a warm, seductive flavour and aroma. It is an important ingredient and is used in a variety of food preparations, both sweet and savoury.

Cassia

Similar to cinnamon, Cassia has a more pungent, bittersweet flavour. It is sold as bark and buds. The bark is more difficult to grind than cinnamon. If you can't find cassia, substitute with cinnamon.

Chat Masala

A beige-coloured ground spice blend with a tangy flavour, this is a combination of dried ginger, black pepper, red chillies, coriander, cumin and black salt. It is easily available from Asian food shops and the recommended brand is MDH.

Chana Masala Powder

A wonderful tart, tangy and aromatic homemade spice blend for curries, especially chickpeas. The recommended brand is MDH.

Chillies

We use long, thin green chillies that are available in supermarkets as well as Asian food shops. I prefer Kashmiri Red chillies for their great depth of flavour and colour. These are big and broad and are used whole or powdered. The recommended brand is FUDCO.

Cloves

A small, nail-shaped spice, cloves derive their name from the French word cloud, meaning "nail". It is one of the spices used in garam masala and curry mixes.

Coccum/Kodumpuli/Malabar Tamarind

After the fruit is harvested, the thick outer rind is sundried until it turns dark and shrivels. It can then be stored for years and used when needed. Almost odorless, coccum is faintly sweet and extremely sour, with a unique smokey flavour that is predominantly used in Keralan seafood dishes.

Coconut

Fresh coconut is an important ingredient in Keralan cooking. The white flesh can be grated, finely sliced or shredded. It can also be toasted or deep fried. You can roughly whiz the chopped flesh in a blender or mini food processor to grate it without reducing it to a paste. In this form, coconut freezes well with little loss of flavour. You can also buy fresh coconut chunks in supermarkets.

Coconut – Desiccated

Desiccated coconut is a grated, dried (3% moisture content max.) and unsweetened fresh meat, or kernel, from a mature coconut. Desiccated coconuts are graded by their cutting size, for example, fine grade and medium grade. Fine grade has a smaller particle size than the medium grade.

Coconut Milk

This is prepared from fresh coconut flesh but I recommend Maggi Coconut milk powder, which can be blended with warm water to improve the consistency of a sauce.

Coconut Oil

This is extracted from coconut flesh and because of its high saturated fat content it is solid at room temperature. I often use it for tempering and when cooking seafood. It is sold in super markets.

Coriander

The fresh leaves are called cilantro and also used for cooking. The spice is also used in herbal oils and medicines. Both coriander and cilantro are aromatic and strongly flavoured. Coriander seeds, powdered or whole, are used in curries; the leaves are used for chutneys, curries or as a garnish.

Cumin

Cumin has antispasmodic, sedative and antibacterial properties. Like most spices, cumin has an aromatic and spicy flavour, intensifying in taste when heated. It can be used in whole for tempering and in powder form in curries and chutneys.

Curry Leaves

Curry leaves are not to be confused with the ground spice mixture known as curry. My recipes always use fresh leaves, which you can buy from Asian food shops. Freezing curry leaves preserves their flavour very well. Curry leaves have a mild aroma and flavour, which is enhanced further when heated in oil. Curry leaves are used in seasoning oil with mustard seeds and other accompaniments and in curries, chutneys, and vegetable dishes. They are an essential ingredient in authentic Keralan cuisine.

Dried Mango Powder (Amchur Powder)

Tangy and sour tasting, this is made from slices of green, unripe mangoes that are powdered. It is used as a flavouring and souring agent in sauces and salad dressings. You might find this labelled as Amchoor and the recommended brand is MDH

Fenugreek Leaves (Kasoori Methi)

Fenugreek leaves taste very different from fenugreek seeds and the two are are not interchangeable. Crumble the dried leaves into recipes or else powder them.

Fenugreek Seeds

The flavour of fenugreek is bitter, strong and faintly sweet. In Keralan cuisine, the seeds are used in fish curries and pickles.

Garlic

Sold fresh-in-the-bulb, garlic can be separated into cloves and fresh cloves can be chopped, sliced or made into a paste. Garlic also stores well as a powder.

Garam Masala

The blended spice powder is usually added to dishes towards the end of cooking. The recipe varies according to the region but typically it contains cardamom, cinnamon, cloves, cumin and black pepper. I have developed my own blend of Garam Masala.

Ghee

This clarified butter has long been the main cooking medium of India. However, the growing awareness of healthy eating means vegetable oil is taking its place. It is sold in supermarkets and Asian food shops.

Ginger

It is believed to have originated in India, though early travellers carried the root to every corner of the earth. Ginger has several medicinal properties and is used in home remedies. Use it chopped, julienned or in a paste.

Gram Flour

Also called besan or chick pea flour, this is a fine flour made from ground chickpeas. It is pale yellow in colour and has an excellent nutty flavour and is used in batters.

Green Mango

Used in recipes for their contribution of sourness in curries, look for the small green firm ones. Peel the skin off and the discard the seeds. They are available in Asian shops.

Jaggery

Jaggery is a coarse, unrefined sugar from the sugar cane plant. It has a distinctive taste and is much less sweet than refined sugar. It is used to enrich sauces, chutneys and desserts.

Kitchen King

Kitchen King is a blend of spice powder, available in Asian super markets and recommended brand is MDH

Madras Curry Powder

Curry powder is a spice mixture of widely varying composition developed by the British during the days of the Raj as a means of approximating the taste of Indian cuisine at home. Curry powders are often coriander, cumin, fenugreek, mustard, chili, black pepper and salt.

Mustard

The black whole seeds compensate with a flavour that is intense and pungent. Mustard seeds are ground to a paste in certain dishes but are more often used as a seasoning in hot oil.

Nutmeg/Mace

Once harvested, the ripe fruit that encases the hard brown nut is removed, and the lacey red covering known as mace is separated and dried. Mace has a delicate flavour and fragrance and is used in garam masala powder, rice dishes etc. Ground nutmeg in used in sweet dishes and savouries.

Onions

These are a staple. Brown onions, in general, have quite a strong flavour but also impart a good texture to curries and sauces. Red onions are milder and sweeter. They are fantastic for pickling and added a dash of colour to salads.

Paneer/ Indian Cottage Cheese

Paneer is a very mild, fresh Indian cheese, made by curdling hot milk with lemon juice or diluted vinegar before letting the whey drain off through a muslin-lined sieve. The remaining solids are lightly pressed until firm enough to hold their shape, after which the cheese can be cut for cooking. It has a rather bland taste but is good to use with sauces and spice mixes. It is available in Asian shops.

Poppy Seeds

White poppy seeds are used to add crunch and a slightly nutty flavour, or finely ground to add to various spice powders.

Rosewater

Rosewater is a by-product from the manufacture of rose oil. Its distinctive, perfumed flavour is used in desserts and biryani. Be sure to buy rosewater, which is milder than extract.

Saffron

This expensive ingredient is the stigma of a specific crocus flower. The stigmas can only be picked by hand and it takes 250,000 stigmas to make just half a kilo of saffron, hence its high price. Powder the saffron and mix with water. It can be used for flavouring.

Shallots/ Madras Onions

Shallots are similar in appearance to baby onions but they are more oval in shape and the flesh is pink. Due to their high pungency, raw shallots have a more pronounced taste than onions. When a shallot is sautéed the sugars caramelize. This gives the shallots a sweeter, unique taste.

Soft Shell Crab

Soft shell crab is a culinary term for crabs which have recently molted their old exoskeleton and are still soft. Soft shells are removed from the water as soon as they molt to prevent any hardening of their shell. This means that almost the entire animal can be eaten, rather than having to shell the animal to reach the meat. The exceptions are the mouthparts, the gills and the abdomen, which must be discarded. The remaining, edible part of the crab is typically deep fried or sautéed.

Tamarind

Available as whole fruit, ground or in a paste, tamarind has a fairly sour odor and a sweet-and-sour flavour. It is used in curries and chutneys.

Tapioca

Cassava, often referred to as tapioca from its word in Portuguese, is widely consumed in the Indian state of Kerala, usually as breakfast or in the evening. It is boiled after skinning and cutting it into large pieces. Mashed tapioca is paired with meat or fish curry, especially sardines.

Tomato

Use fresh tomatoes, really ripe sweet tomatoes, then chop them with their skin and seeds. I have also used tinned tomatoes in some recipes. They give a good color. Tomato paste can also be used and that gives a good consistency to curries and chutneys.

Toor Dal

Similar to channa dal but much smaller, these disintegrate when cooked.

Turmeric

Turmeric has a faintly medicinal flavour and aroma. It is known to be a natural antiseptic and blood purifier as well as a potential antioxidant. Its used along with other ingredients to make curries.

Urad Dal Split

These are black gram lentils, protein-rich pulses that are sold hulled and split. The beans are, in fact, creamy white in color; it's just their skin that is black. These whole black lentils are harder to digest than some lentils but are delicious when cooked well.

Useful equipment

Food Processor

This helps in cutting, slicing, chopping or blending.

Grater

Helps in finely grating boiled potatoes.

Hand Blender

Allows you to purée quickly without the need to transfer into a separate blender or pan. For example, if you want to purée soup, you can blend in a saucepan rather than tipping to another vessel.

Also consider how fast the hand blender is and what attachments come with it. And if you're going to use it to blend colourful fruit and veg, like tomatoes, you might want to go for a stainless steel model as plastic can stain easily.

You want the blender to be able to blitz a thick soup. But if you use it too quickly for delicate jobs, like making mayonnaise, the mixture will curdle. So use sensible speeds.

Kadai

This is a big round bottomed vessel with two handles, similar to a wok. The round bottom spreads the heat evenly through the base and into the food. It is ideal for sautéing and deep frying.

Measuring Jug

To measure liquid in milliliters (ml).

Mortar and Pestle

This is not essential but crushing or bruising spices by using a mortar and pestle gives effective results and a distinct flavour dishes.

Oven

This is essential. Tandoor – or clay ovens – are used in some dishes, though a pre-heated conventional oven is a robust substitute.

Pans

Stainless steel thick-bottomed pans are used for cooking curries for a long time. Non-stick pans are used for pan frying and tempering.

Pacojet

Pacojet is a kitchen appliance for professionals that micro-purees deep-frozen foods into ultra-fine textures (such as mousses, sauces and sorbets) without thawing. Manufactured in Switzerland, the Pacojet is sold worldwide for hotel, restaurant and catering gastronomy.

Scales

Every kitchen should have a digital scale. They are inexpensive and can measure quantities in grams. I would highly recommend using when you try out my recipes.

Sieves

Sieves are made of wire mesh and are designed with one long handle. The better ones have a hook or a loop that rests on the rim of a pot or bowl, making it more convenient to collect strained liquid. The bowl of a sieve can be rounded or cone shaped.

Sieves are usually referred to as coarse- or fine-meshed. You'll find yourself using a coarse-mesh sieve for most everyday tasks, from straining small amounts of stock to sifting flour or other dry ingredients. When it comes to making exquisitely clear soup or a very refined sauce, you will want a fine-mesh sieve – one that eliminates all lumps or any hint of graininess.

Spice Grinder

Small electric coffee grinders are available and are best for freshly ground spices. Take care not to overload them. Once grinded, keep the lid closed or transfer spices powders to an airtight container so the aromas are retained.

Recipe index

A

B

Basil paste 215
Basmati rice 134
Beef and cabbage - Rosily Aunty 104
Beef - Bombay Frankie roll 190
Beef kurumelagu 166
Beef stew 164
Beetroot cake and dal shorba 54
Beetroot pachadi 222
Beetroot, pickled 219
Bell pepper (red) sauce 221
Bhel puri 73
Bhuno besan 222
Boatman fish curry 120
Boiled, grated potatoes 223
Bombay chat 73
Braised egg - Mom 102
Brioche Buns 225

C

Calamari 78
Chappati 217
Chatpata sauce 214
Cheese samosa (4 pieces) 76
Chef Siddartha laal maas 142
Chicken - Bombay Frankie roll 194
Chicken, Kerala style 198
Chicken pakoda and tomato rasam 58
Chicken tikka connoisseur 70
Chicken tikka red marinade 217
Chick pea and potato mash 224
Chilli (red) paste 223
Chocomosa 205
Coconut chilli prawns 122
Coconut, garlic, chilli spice powder (ghati spice) 219
Coconut ice-cream 212
Coconut paste 222
Coconut soup and cabbage cake 50
Coconut water and Malibu sorbet 206
Confit duck legs 224
Crab 66
Crab cake 66
Crab salad 68
Crab, soft shell 69
Creme brulee, rose 210
Crème brulee, garam masala 211
Curry leaf and garlic paste 223

D

Dal shorba 54
Dal Tadka 174
Duck legs, confit 65

E

Egg, Braised - Mom 102

F

Flour Mix - batter 225
Fish (green) curry - Chef William 110
Fresh from the creamery 74
Fried garlic 218
Fried onion 217

G

Garam Masala crème brulee 211
Garam masala powder 134, 211, 216
Garam masala powder - Keralan Style 216
Garlic, fried 218
Ghati spice 219
Ginger garlic paste 221
Goat's cheese and pickled beetroot salad 77
Grated potatoes 223
Green fish curry - chef William 110

H

Hara (basil) 71
Homestyle chicken curry 156
Hung yoghurt 219

I

J

K

Kadai masala powder 219
Kappa meen 93
Kashmiri roganjosh 136
Keema Pao with quail eggs 83
Keralan homestyle lamb curry 146
Kerala style fried chicken 198
Khorma sauce 163

L

Lamb 80
Lamb Pattice 82
Lamb biryani, Malabar 132
Lamb curry, Keralan homestyle 146
Lamb ularthiyathu (lamb coconut fry) 144
Loin of lamb 150

M

Makhani sauce 215

Malabar fish curry 128
Malabar lamb biryani 132
Malabar prawns 84
Malai (creamy cheese) 71
Mint chutney 215
Mint sauce 220
Mint sorbet 221
Mixed berry sauce 222
Mixed salad leaves 221
Mom, braised egg 102
Murgh kofta khorma 162
Murg tikka lababdar 160

N

Nadan tharavu roast - Pushpy Aunty 108
Nawabi murg 154

O

Onion, fried 217
Onion masala 191
Onion, red, and cucumber, pickled 224

P

Paneer chatpata 184
Paneer kofta Makhani 180
Paneer tikka 74
Pao - brioche buns 225
Passion fruit and chilli dressing 220
Passion fruit and chilli sorbet 207
Pear chutney 218
Pickled beetroot 219
Pickled red onion and cucumber 224
Pidi and tharavu 62
Pidi (rice dumpling) 64
Pistachio ice-cream 204
Pork vindalu 168
Potato 182
Potatoes, boiled/grated 223
Potato cake and chana masala 72
Prawn moilee 126
Prawns 84, 122
Prawn samosa 86
Punjabi chana masala 176, 216
Pushpy Aunty - nadan tharavu roast, 108

Q

R

Raan akbari 138
Red bell pepper sauce 221
Red chilly 71
Red chilli paste 223
Rice 186
Rice, basmati 134
Risotto, seafood 125

Rose creme brulee 210
Rose petal ice-cream 208
Rosily Aunty - beef and cabbage – 104

S

Saag khumb 172
Salad dressing 225
Salmon 88
Salmon cake 90
Salmon pickle 89
Samosa pastry 223
Savoy cabbage, carrot and runner bean thoran 178
Sea bass pollichathu 118
Seafood risotto 125
Seekh kebab 80
Shyama Aunty - vegetable stew 106
Soft shell crab 69
Streets of mumbai 72
Sweetened yoghurt 219

T

Tamarind chutney 220
Tandoori chicken 158
Tandoori king prawn 87
Tandoori king prawns and seafood risotto 124
Tandoori salmon 88
Tomato chutney 218
Tomato rasam 60

U

Ulli chutney 220

V

Vada pao 196
Vanilla ice-cream 212
Vegetable stew - Shayama Aunty 106
Venison pao 200

W

William - Green fish curry - Chef 110

X

Y

Yoghurt, hung, 219
Yoghurt, sweetened 219

Z

Thanks

I thank everyone who helped me along this journey and taught me discipline, respect, patience and how to cook good food.

Siddaratha Rathore, my head chef and my line chefs: Leela, Waquar, Ashish, Mani, Amar, Arjun who helped me with the food trails for the recipes. A special mention to my front of house staff, Raman Bijalwan and Adam Sharieff. Thank you.

Peter Acton, my PR man and good friend, for the great support and help through the most difficult times. Without your help I would not be here now. Thank you for the title of the book 'The 5000 Mile Journey.

Special mention to Joshy Manjummel for the wonderful photography in Kerala, and Shahin Edward for the design of the front cover and logistical support in Kerala.

Roger, Laxmi and Rupali, who spent endless hours proof reading.

Thanks to David Briggs for the editorial production and design of the book.

A big thank you to Andy Richardson, for your vision and for making the book a reality. Without your commitment and help this book would never have happened.